S.M. Minasian

Correspondence and Other Documents

Relating to the troubles in the Turkish missions of the American Board,

C.F.M.

S.M. Minasian

Correspondence and Other Documents
Relating to the troubles in the Turkish missions of the American Board, C.F.M.

ISBN/EAN: 9783337289188

Printed in Europe, USA, Canada, Australia, Japan

Cover: Foto ©Suzi / pixelio.de

More available books at **www.hansebooks.com**

CORRESPONDENCE

AND OTHER DOCUMENTS RELATING TO

THE

TROUBLES IN THE TURKISH MISSIONS

OF THE

AMERICAN BOARD,

C. F. M.

SUBMITTED TO MEMBERS OF THE BOARD

BY S. M. MINASIAN,

WITH A PREFACE

BY REV. LEONARD WOOLSEY BACON, D. D.

NEW YORK:

PRINTED BY ATKIN & PROUT,

1882.

TABLE OF CONTENTS.

PREFACE.

I have had only a brief time to look at the contents of the following pamphlet, in the proof sheets, before writing a preface to it. I am glad, on the whole, that I did not see it earlier, for I should have been tempted to propose some changes in it, in the arrangement of the materials, and to add something in the way of argument and application. But it is better as it is—a mere collection of papers which the Protestant Christians of the Turkish Empire represented by Mr. Minasian desire to lay before the members of the American Board of Commissioners for Foreign Missions as necessary to the full understanding of their case. It is safe to say that the Board will give a generous and considerate attention to an appeal from the policy of its Executive proceeding from such a source ; and that the unfortunate indiscretion, hastily committed a year ago on the part of the Executive, in attempting to prevent such a communication from coming to the knowledge of the Board, will not be repeated.

The letters from Armenian pastors and church-members will make on most readers a strong impression, first, of the intelligence and good spirit of the writers ; it will be obvious that we have to do with clear-headed and Christian gentlemen. Secondly, it will be seen that they write under grievous burdens of poverty, trouble and anxiety. It will require no small effort of imagination on our part to put ourselves in their place. They belong to a nation without a country—the very oldest of the Christian nations, now living under the intolerable yoke of infidel conquerors, and crushed into the dust by burdens of misgovernment. They love the truth of Christ—how well they love it, some of them have shown by proofs such as it rarely falls to any of us to give. And they also love, with an affectionate patriotism that is deepened by her sorrows, their homeless nation, their kindred according to the flesh. The cause of Christ and his truth, and the interests of their beloved people, both seem to them in danger of ruin from an unwise policy on the part of the Executive and missionaries of the American Board ; and from that policy they appeal to the Board itself, which is the proper Court of Appeal, and whose proper function it is, each year, in all the light that it can get from whatever quarter, to review the administration of its Executive and control its policy. On questions of policy we may dissent from the views of the Armenian brethren. What our judgment on the whole case is going to be, after the fuller light which we are waiting for, none of us ought to pretend to know at present. But that we shall fail to give the most kindly, patient and unstinted hearing to everything that these brethren wish to say, out of their " continual sorrow of heart," their deep poverty and their faithful service, now that after many delays and hindrances they have at last reached the ear of the Board—this is not credible of such a body of American Christians.

Mr. Minasian has (unexpectedly to me) appended to his pamphlet three articles of mine, written just after the meeting at Portland, and published at long intervals afterward in *The Independent*. I am glad he has reprinted them. They were written with an earnest and single desire to help toward a right solution of pending questions, and I believe they are substantially sound. This view is confirmed by a very gratifying letter of approval addressed to me from one of the Prudential Committee, and still more by the answers that have been made to the articles. One answer, by a recently returned missionary, complains that I " misrepresent the Western Turkey mission in some important particulars," and then proceeds, quite unconsciously, to confirm my statements on every point of fact on which he testifies. Our old friend, Dr. Wood, of Constantinople, repels the imputation of a lack of frank dealing toward the Board on the part of its Executive, by charging it to a Rip Van Winkle somnolency or dullness in me. I am too painfully conscious of my own defects to deny the charge, to which my remembrance of the Doctor's own wide-awake vivacity on

4

missionary subjects gives double poignancy. But it is really hardly fair for him, in the con
sciousness of his own exuberant animation, to reproach his less gifted brethren. Some con
sideration must be shown, in dealing with so large a public, for that class of sleepy-heads to
which I am so unfortunate to belong. It is possible, however, that the good Doctor's personal observation of public assemblies, in his experience as a public speaker in America,
may have led him to exaggerated ideas of the sleepiness of the general public.

In closing this Preface, I would emphasize the point, presented elsewhere, that the main
question before the American Board is not that of the Turkish missions, momentous as this
question is. It is the question whether the constitution and authority of the Board are to be
respected by its own officers and employees—whether the annual meeting of the Board is to be
steered and controlled by the Executive, or whether the Executive is to be controlled by the
annual meeting—whether parties alleging objection or grievance against the Executive,
such as missionaries, mission-churches or contributors, are to have prompt hearing for their
complaint, or are to hang on the consent of the opposite party—whether, in short, the noble
constitution of the Board is to lapse, through habitual though unintended encroachments on
the part of its Executive.

I am strongly convinced that this question will not be rightly settled except by the safe,
simple and easy course of confiding the arrangements for the business of the annual meeting
of the Board to a special committee.

LEONARD WOOLSEY BACON.

NORWICH, Conn., September 15, 1883.

CORRESPONDENCE

AND OTHER DOCUMENTS RELATING TO THE TROUBLES IN THE TURKISH MISSIONS OF THE A. B. C. F. M.

LETTER TO THE MISSIONARIES.

PROVIDENCE, R. I., December 22, 1882.

DEAR BROTHER: You are doubtless aware that a committee was appointed by the Board at its late meeting in Portland, to examine to the bottom the grounds of the differences between the missionaries in Western Turkey and some of the Armenian brethren, and to suggest the needful remedies.

That committee has had one meeting, and appointed me to act for them In this correspondence. I need not assure you of the kind feelings of al the committee, or our satisfaction in having the privilege of doing something that may tend to promote the kingdom of Christ in Western Asia. In behalf of the committee, I write for information from you as an individual on the following topics, viz :

1. The origin and present condition of the trouble. Is it likely to pass away if treated judiciously?

2. The claims of the Armenian brethren in connection with the disbursement of missionary funds.

3. The methods and extent of mutual co-operation between you and them.

4. The exodus of graduates of our missionary seminaries and of pastors to other countries, and especially to the United States.

5. Does the alleged feeling of caste exist among our missionaries, and what has occasioned that imputation?

6. What is the prospect of the speedy completion of foreign missionary work among the Armenians and how is it to be brought about?

7. In the present aspect of the matter, would a deputation from this country be desirable?

We should be happy also to hear from you on any other points which you deem it important for us to know in order to enable us to render the best possible service to Christ in this matter.

After you have written to us as an individual, we would like to hear from your station as such, on the same topics, and also from the Western Turkey mission.

We shall also write for information to some of the Armenian brethren.

In behalf of, and at the request of the committee,

Your fellow-servant,   T. LAURIE.

TO THE ARMENIANS.

PROVIDENCE, R. I., December, 1882.

DEAR SIR: Though personally strangers, yet I trust we are members of one blessed family, whose head is Christ. It is one of the privileges of my life, which I never recall without thankfulness, that I was permitted to be present at the organization of the first Evangelical Armenian Church, of which the beloved Apisoghom was Pastor, and one of my most delightful anticipations of heaven is to meet that great multitude, which no man can number, redeemed to God by the blood of Christ, out of every kindred, and tongue, and people, and nation, and spend eternity with them in beholding the glory of our Redeemer.

Dearly beloved brethren have gone out from us to make known the great love wherewith Christ has loved us, and you have received them as angels of God. Some of them are now worshipping along with some of your people before the throne of God and of the Lamb, but it grieves us to hear that other plants have sprung up in the garden of God along with his pleasant fruits, and that there is a coldness between some of your people and some of the missionaries.

The churches, which sent out the missionaries, grieve over this state of things, and at the late Annual Meeting of the American Board at Portland appointed the Hon. William Hyde, of Massachusetts; Hon. J. B. Page, ex-Governor of Vermont; Z. Styles Ely, Esq., of New York; Hon. A. C. Barstow, ex-Mayor of this city; the Rev. Geo. Leon Walker, D. D., of Hartford, Connecticut; the Rev. Samuel Harris, D. D., Professor of Systematic Theology in the Seminary at New Haven, Connecticut, and myself, a committee to examine to the bottom the grounds of difference and to suggest the needful remedies. We desire to do all that in us lies to heal these wounds of the body of Christ, and in order to know best how to do it, we seek information on the subject from you and from the missionaries.

So we come to you as to a brother in Christ asking you to tell us all about it. We do not propose particular questions, but want you to tell us all that is a source of trouble to you, or if you have nothing to complain of yourself, tell us what others complain about, and tell us fully, for we believe that the more thoroughly we search into the trouble, the better we shall be able to arrange for its relief.

We would like also to have your own idea of the best method for its removal, for, though we have this treasure in earthen vessels, yet we also know that those who are in Christ have learned of Him who is meek and owly in heart, and so we have good hope that one and all of them shall receive rest to their souls.

If in any way we can minister to your spiritual good, and that of the churches which God has planted among you, we shall thank God who gives us to enjoy a privilege so blessed.

Please excuse the printing of this letter, as my hands are full of work, and I send it to many others as well as to yourself.

In behalf of the committee, and at its request, I write this, and subscribe myself.   Yours, for Christ's sake,   THOMAS LAURIE.

ADA BAZAR, Asia Minor, Turkey, April 2, 1883.

Rev. Thomas Laurie, D.D.:

DEAR SIR: We hailed with pleasure the appointment of a committee by the last annual meeting of the A. B. C. F. M. in Portland, Me., to take into consideration the anxious desires of the Evangelical Armenian churches in Turkey, for the building up of Zion. While looking with the deepest interest for the result, we received your very kind and courteous letter, which disappointed us of our expectations; for we see that neither is the question well understood, nor is the mode of treatment satisfactory to us. Truly angelic men from America—as your letter says—came to preach the pure gospel to us. Thank God for it. Through the preaching of the word we were awakened, and have seen the ultimate aim of Christianity. Thank God for it. Thanks to the American churches. Thanks to the missionaries. Nay ! no " other plants have sprung up in the garden of God." No ! there is no *personal* " coldness between some of our people and some of the missionaries." No ! we have no personal troubles and quarrels with any one and anywhere. We maintain that the facts are entirely opposed to your statement.

The question is this—ought we to think that the American Christian deems it incompatible with love and gratitude when the Armenian—being taught of them—is more earnest to save his own people, and to repair the waste places of his Zion—that Zion for the standing of which the native has labored and suffered with tears and bleeding. For this cause the Armenian Protestant is exiled out of his community and church; entirely deprived of his inheritance and institutions ; and for this cause sainted Apisoghom—kindly mentioned in your letter—and others were martyred. Are these our aspirations for the elevation of our people incompatible with our devotion to you and to the missionaries, while this country is in a great crisis? We were rather thinking that you would be grieved if there were no such agitations and complaints, and you would be glad that we are not indifferent and dead tools and hirelings in the hands of the society. Will an affectionate Father look with dislike on the increasing efforts and demands of his maturing son ? Which is the best, to have a river which sometimes overflows, or to have a stagnant pond that brings forth death ? Every good movement will have some irregularity, if there is any in ours.

We do not think it necessary to repeat our complaints in this letter, as they are already published to the world. And we are sure that they reached you already through Mr. Minasian, our honored representative, and you could know them if you would. And by and by another official document will be published. Our complaints are, the decay of the former piety of our churches ; the comparatively very small profits that we got from an immense labor of forty long years ; the ruin threatening our posterity. God forbid that you should be passive, or putting charges of petty quarrels to our doors, while here we are in a heart-rending condition, and in agony, and shedding bloody tears while popery and infidelity are threatening to swallow up the country with open jaws. Our complaint is on a question between death and life, and not on personal questions or " coldness." We surely hope that you will do your best, and lend us a helping hand as soon as possible, as you expect comfort at the last day, for the great God will judge Boards and Managers, as well as individuals. Remember, dear sir, that our business here is not with a heathen country, nor even with a Roman Catholic one. Our work is to revive spiritual Christianity in a Christian church of an existence of many centuries. The Armenians of the old church ought to find us their superiors in every way. Our elevated and improved position might invite others to join our community. But the general policy of the Board has thrown obstacles in the way. The arbitrary control of the foreign missionary puts us in a position that our old Armenian friends look upon us as a *handful* of *worthless renegades*, who sold ourselves to the foreigners for selfish ends, and this is all and the only source of our troubles and grievances.

After speaking thus much of our complaints, allow us to tell something of the complaints of others of us. Missionaries of the Board have no sympathy with those of our young men who go to America. You are not ignorant of the present lamentable condition of this country. Is it a matter of wonder that our young men who received light from you become over fond of America, the source of light ? Why! the Chinese and the Japanese do the same. We are rather surprised that so few of our select men go from us to America. Nine out of ten of those who went to America and returned have been useful men amongst us, and leaders to elevation, both by counsel and work and contributions. We would have been better off if some of them, unfortunately, had not turned their backs, disgusted by the treatment of the missionaries, who represented them as being unprincipled and faithless mercenary deceivers. The hand that worked for their mental development seems to try to crush their attempts towards mental and social elevation. It is objected that they are becoming burdens on the charity of the American Christians. Why, let that community withhold their charity if they could and would ! But, fortunately, neither the missionaries nor we natives are the judges and directors of that Christ-like sympathy that flows from the American headquarters throughout the world and through every channel.

Another point : Whenever we bring forth our complaints, the missionaries, both here and in America, throw to our teeth always the same charge, that *money* and the handling of the treasures of the Board are our sole object. This is altogether wrong, and we protest to death and forever against this foul charge. In the mean time, it ought not to be overlooked that money is a secondary thing, and a valuable servant if used for the work ; but if it is a weapon in the hands of him who holds it turned against the right management of the work, then it is a curse. There is also another important point here to be mentioned in this connection. The greatest and most difficult part of the work is accomplished through native agency-pioneer work is always done with the natives ; nor can we deny that the humblest Armenian Protestant has done his best for the work, with all his might and property and life. In one word, all the work is ours, and if the pecuniary help given to us in Christian charity will always be held to our face as a reproach, on the other hand, it must not be forgotten that the missionary also could do nothing without the native, and the work would be totally paralyzed. The natives, with their hundred churches and congregations, in their extreme poverty contribute from twenty to thirty thousand dollars for religious and educational purposes. The noble American, observing our struggles, sacrifice and work, will he not help us, giving as much in this gigantic undertaking ? We know the Americans—we know them from our own personal experience ; we know their Christian spirit and generosity ; we know that he is willing and ready to do the more.

At last, dear sir, we object to your mode of treatment, and this for two reasons. If you will look at the cause and nature of these complaints by the answers of individuals, and form your judgment according to their personal opinions, we fear that you will seem to ignore the just rights of our feeble churches, and confirm the natives in their suspicions that the Board holds a policy that has never taken into consideration the rights of the churches, but cares only for its own interests. And from this source arise the conflicts between the native and the missionary. Remember the eagle that stole a coal from the altar, and thereby set her nest on fire, which consumed both her young eagles and herself.

Second. Yours is not a natural method. We ask to be judged as churches, according to ecclesiastical methods of procedure, with any sort of ecclesiastical council or court. If not, who will decide the question ? Can a committee chosen by the Board do this work ? For there is a great dissimilarity between the Board and these churches.

We will try to describe our idea with an example very familiar to us We often make the hen sit on duck's eggs. She hatches ducklings, who naturally run away from their mother into the water. Of course the mother hen is very kind and fond of them, and runs after them cackling and very much confused, fearing that her brood is in danger of drowning. But we all know very well that the kind old mother hen is not a competent authority in this matter from her peculiar stand-point.

But if all these appeals will go for naught, we confidently leave our cause to the judgment and good sense of the Christian public. The Americans are our models in every good thing, and we are sure that they will not despise us, weak and puny though we are, as they are lovers of fair play in every case.

May the grace of our Lord be with you, and the other honored Christian gentlemen of the committee. Amen.

We remain, dear sir, your obedient servants and co-laborers in Christ.

ALEXANDER DJIJIZIAN, Pastor.

S. C. KAVALGIAN, M. D., Elder.

FROM REV. KEROPE YAKOBIAN.

CÆSAREA, February 23, 1883.

Rev. Thomas Laurie, D.D. :

DEAR SIR : In your printed letter, bearing the date December 15, 1882, your expressions of Christian love and affection have caused us very much joy. We thank God that in the far distant part of the world, on the other side of the ocean, He has prepared Christian brethren who think of us and who pray for us ; and we believe that they and we, all of us, belong to the one family of faith. We have the same Heavenly Father, the same Saviour, the same hope and the same object of life.

You express the desire on the part of your honorable committee to know the causes of the present differences between the missionaries and the native Christians, in order that you may find out some means of removing them. The following, in my opinion, are some of the causes of the differences :

First. We, as a simple Evangelical Church, are beset by many difficulties, and have various needs. We are obliged to protect ourselves against the attacks from without, and at the same time to keep our organization in good order, and we use every means for the advancement of the kingdom of Christ among us. The object and the duty of this church is the reformation of our country, the progress of our nation, the enlightenment of individuals, and the furtherance of the kingdom of Christ. Our church considers it her duty to use every means for the present and future benefit of herself and her descendants ; and hence would consider it unfaithful to her call and injurious to her growth to become indifferent and leave al these things to other hands.

Within the Armenian nation and this evangelical church there is another agency, namely, the missionaries, working for the advancement of the cause of Christ. The object of these two organizations is the enlightenment of one nation, the strengthening of one church ; and the furtherance of the kingdom of God in one country. But these two organizations in their deliberations and decisions are free and independent of each other. There is no connecting link between them ; there is no division of labor among them. From the very foundation of the Evangelical Armenian Church, 37 years ago, no pastor or delegate in behalf of the Armenian Evangelical Union has been admitted to the meetings of the Western Mission when they had discussions regarding the Armenian nation and the Evangelical Church. You may easily imagine how many difficulties and differences may come out of such an arrangement.

Second. Intelligent and able young men who have a desire in their hearts to work for Christ, seeing that the missionaries treat those who work with them as hired assistants, are reluctant to enter the work ; and if they do enter it they leave it very soon.

Third. The Protestant elementary schools are not superior to the Greek and Armenian schools, and in many places are inferior to them. As to the condition of the high schools and seminaries, I may refer you to the very clear explanation contained in the letter of Dr. C. Hamlin in the pamphlet called "Controversy."

Fourth. You will see, in the pamphlet just referred to, a letter containing a decision of the Central Union in regard to the expediency and usefulness of sending able and intelligent young men to the universities and theological halls of Europe and America. The Union have come to this decision, in the belief that young men thus educated would be more useful to our church and country. It causes us great sorrow and regret to see that some of the missionaries oppose such a plan, and that others keep silent. Such conduct seems to be opposed to our rights and freedom, and discourages the able and intelligent young men from any undertaking for the benefit of the country and the church. It is impossible for us not to feel sorrow for such a policy.

These are some causes of the differences which we deplore very much. For the removal of these differences and for the re-establishment of harmony between the missionaries and the Unions, I propose the following remedies to your honorable committee :

First. For the furtherance of the kingdon of Christ among the Armenians in Turkey, it is necessary to pay more attention to the subject of Christian education. In this way, the greatest need being supplied, the majority of the complaints would be removed, and able and educated young men being prepared in the Evangelical Church, it would cause great joy to the natives as well as to the missionaries, and its natural result would be harmony and love between the natives and the missionaries.

Second. Let there be a mixed committee composed of missionaries and of men elected by the Unions, to decide regarding the means to be employed for the reformation of the Armenians, such as Christian literature, schools, higher schools, colleges, and theological halls, and the curriculum to be gone through in each. In such co-operation with the missionaries the native members would acquire experience in conducting such business, and when the board withdraws its missionaries from the field, the church will have able and experienced men to carry on the work begun, and such a step will be agreeable to the Protestant communities in this country.

Third. It is desirable and urgent that the missionaries belonging to a station, and the pastors of the church in that station, should decide together and with equal voice regarding the work affecting the churches and mission stations, and that they should decide who should go to the universities and theological halls of Europe and America to get theological and medical training. In this way the missionaries and the pastors would come nearer

to each other and understand each other better, and the result would be
real co-operation, and both parties would be encouraged in their respective
works.

Fourth. If the churches in America and more especially the American
Board would occasionally condescend to hear the desires and the plans of
the clergy of the Evangelical Armenian church, for the advancement of the
cause of Christ in Turkey, the rights and the freedom of the churches being
in this way recognized, they would be encouraged in their work.

Having taken the liberty of expressing my thoughts and desires to your
honorable committee, I leave them to your high decisions, and praying for
the help of God for the success of your committee, I remain your brother
in Christ, KEROPÉ YAKOBIAN, Pastor.

FROM REV. D. G. GARABEDIAN.

BROOSA, Turkey, December, 30, 1882.

If the proposed deputation from America is to be composed of those
who only regard the interests of the American Board, it will be utterly
useless, or if they draw their information from new, inexperienced
persons, who do not at all understand the questions, it
will be equally useless. There is fear that our inexperienced young
preachers, depending upon the missionaries for their support and knowing
nothing about the questions, may take their part. Rev. Mr. Baldwin has
on several occasions threatened us, saying that the Bithynia Union (and
Mr. Minasian) has done them great injury in America ; hence, he says, they
will not be able to give us the needed aid this year. He tries in this way
to mislead the people and induce them to protest against the doings of the
Bithynia Union. May God, who is the judge and Lord over all, deliver
our people from such tyranny! That wicked mammon, which rules the
earth, they wish to make it also rule in religious matters. "One who has
no money can have no rights!" I was much grieved to hear that Pastor
Simon has resigned. To be left, in his advanced age, after forty years'
labor, in his unfortunate position, is extremely trying. His withdrawal
from the field at this moment, when important questions are to be discussed,
is a serious loss to the work, as very few of us can have the experience
he possesses. Our church also has come to that state that it cannot sustain itself. Some of its well-to-do members are lately deceased, and others
have become embarrassed in the general business crisis of the country.
The trustees of the church deliberating upon this matter asked Mr. Baldwin to aid them in order to make up the deficit of the year. Mr. Baldwin,
referring to the late occurrences in America, told them he could not do it.
The people are looking upon the state of things with growing despair—
their organization is not satisfactory at all, neither are they able to sustain it.

Those who comprehend the tottering state of the work entertain grave
apprehensions. You may infer from the account given that my remaining
here is quite doubtful, and if I leave here, do not think I can succeed in

any other place in this country, for the same general reasons. Sometimes I think that compelled by these circumstances I might go to America, there to become a pastor to the German colonists, as about 50 of my classmates in Bale are now pastors there. The Lord knows with what zeal and aspirations I returned to Turkey at the close of my studies in Bale! How long, O Lord, how long!

FROM REV. THOMAS BOYAJIAN.

DIARBEKIR, Turkey, November 17, 1882.

The pamphlet entitled "Controversy," &c., represents very correctly the true state of things. But what good will it do, since neither the missionaries have the desire to be corrected, nor is there any strength left in the people to carry on the battle? I am thoroughly tired of all talking. Protestantism in this land has become as a thing of no account. Popery will eventually, I fear, rule over the people. Already Popish missionaries are filling every part of the country, and by their wise course have accomplished great things and will accomplish still greater. During my absence from here disturbances have been successfully created in my church. Missionaries say they have done nothing, but the brethren state to the contrary. On my return I worked very hard to re-establish peace in the church, and succeeded in a measure. But the state of things made a painful impression upon my mind. Furthermore, the increasing poverty among the people seemed to predict a sad future as to the progress of the work. Our church had two pastors and three schools, besides other work, for which about $1,400 annual expenditure was required. I found that the people would not be able to meet this expenditure any longer. They have not been able to pay my salary for the past three years. If I continued my pastorate it would have been necessary to dismiss the assistant pastor and shut up the schools. It seemed to me best to sacrifice rather my own interests, therefore I sent in my resignation as pastor three months ago. The brethren labored hard to persuade me to recall it, but I did not think it wise to do so. Now the assistant pastor carries on the work, but I still preach regularly, though relieved from official responsibility; and shall continue this to me most pleasing service so long as my time and ability permit. Thus, you see, my dear brother, that I also have been compelled, after twenty-eight years' pastorate, to withdraw from the work. Pastor S——, who you know has faithfully devoted his life to the work, is getting old, and the missionaries do not help him. He receives from his people less than $70 a year; so in his last days he is compelled to live in utter poverty. The pastors of our neighborhood have retired—one to Constantinople and the other to America.

FROM REV. A. M. IKNADIOSIAN.

AINTAB, Turkey, December 6, 1882.

Having heard that a committee was appointed by the American Board to investigate the difficulties in the Turkish Mission, I deem it a duty to tell you what I know about some of the questions.

Some years ago I was sent by the Church at Malatia as a delegate to the meeting of the Harpoot Association, held in Diarbekir. At that meeting complaints against the missionaries were presented. Three years after I was again a delegate at the meeting of the same conference, and found that the complaints of the churches against the missionaries were greatly augmented, and many of the brethren were urging that an appeal should be immediately made directly to the American Board; but we finally succeeded in persuading them to present their appeal to the missionaries in Harpoot, which was afterward done in writing through delegates. But the outcome of the matter was, that the brethren were severely rebuked, and even insulted by the missionaries, and others were secretly persecuted and oppressed in various ways. After this the missionaries tried to have these Association conferences discontinued, and whenever they were held and the discussions referred to the relations of the missionaries to the native churches, they always threatened the brethren.

At a meeting of the churches at Arabkir in 1881, the brethren expressed great dissatisfaction with the conduct of the missionaries, and the general state of things, and felt aggrieved at the tone of Dr. Clark's circular; and were strenuously urging to have issued a public protest against it and expose everything.

But I, with others, using our influence, succeeded again in pacifying them and induced them to confer with the missionaries, and, if possible, to harmonize matters. But our efforts as peacemakers only brought forth a severe rebuke from headquarters in Boston. Many of the rules of the mission, in connection with the school work in the Harpoot field, are arbitrary and obnoxious to the people. The pecuniary assistance which they render may amount to 25 or 30 per cent., and in return for this small percentage they obtain control of the schools and have practically everything under their own management. They carry out this line of action in all the small towns, and among the weak and scattered communities, but in the larger towns, and among more independent communities, they find it quite impracticable. The missionaries have, however, ways for carrying out their own plans, which, according to Dr. Clark, are the best; for instance, they put serious obstacles in the path of those who, in earnestly working for the good of the people, come in contact with their own views and plans. These men are often already weighed down with many difficulties from other sources. Many have, in this way, been driven from the work in disgust and disappointment. I know from my intimate connection with them that many of the pastors in the Harpoot field are in this unfortunate condition. To this cause may be attributed the retirement of Pastor Boyajian, of Diarbekir, Pastor Mardiros, who went to Constantinople for "change of air," and the resignation of the pastor of Kooylou, an important town in the Harpoot field, and also the pastor of Arabgir, who is now abroad trying to raise funds for church building, and who will resign if he does not succeed in his efforts. I myself have been working ten years in Agen. For five years I was pastor of the church there, and had to retire from my work for the same cause, and am now teaching in the college in Aintab. If changes for the better in the workings of the mission are not made soon, others will be driven off in the same way; churches that are neglected and tottering are already not wanting.

I beg you, sir, to look upon these as simple facts, and not as an expression of ill-feeling toward the missionaries; as personally I have rarely had any occasion for complaint, but have received many favors from them, for which I feel under great obligations. Still, under the circumstances, I feel in duty bound to give this information to our Christian friends in America, who have been praying and laboring for these Armenians, who are the only efficient instrument in Divine Providence for the spread of Christian enlightenment and civilization among the various races in Turkey.'

TO THE EVANGELICAL ARMENIAN CHURCHES.

CONSTANTINOPLE, January 30, 1883.

A printed letter signed Thomas Laurie and issued by the committee appointed by the American Board at its last annual meeting, has just been distributed to various persons, inviting the brethren to communicate to said committee their opinions and views respecting the " coldness " which has arisen " between some of your people and some of the missionaries," and which it calls " other plants which have sprung up in the garden of God along with its pleasant fruits."

The Executive Committee of the Bithynia Union, which is appointed by the churches to examine every question affecting their interests, is very glad and thankful to learn that this benevolent society has turned its attention to this most important subject, and has consented to appoint a special committee in order to inquire into the facts and report at its next annual meeting.

But the language and style of this printed letter do not altogether accord with your committee's understanding of the matter. The subject which the Special Committee is to investigate refers, according to our understanding, to our churches, and that too in, as far as concerns the principles of action and their application, whereby the churches and the Lord's work have suffered injury. Our churches and Union honor the reverend missionaries as preachers and ministers of the Word. The question at issue has no reference to individuals personally, or to their moral conduct, as one would conclude from the language of the above mentioned letter. Our churches regard the missionaries as helpful fellow-laborers in spreading the Gospel throughout this noble field. The question raised by the pamphlet does not refer to any dispute between brethren and missionaries arising from any " coldness."

The Union and our churches are on the best personal terms with the reverend missionaries ; they have no quarrel with them, and they commune, pray and labor together. It has often been said on our side that the " suffering of our churches is not personal, but is produced by the retrograde and evil state of the Lord's blessed work."

Your Executive Committee, fearing lest the brethren should take a wrong view of the subject and be led into mistakes which might give rise to personal questions, followed by evil consequences, have thought it proper to impress the following points upon the brethren and churches :

1. The brethren should be very careful lest the questions which belong to the entire community should be mistaken for personal ones, and lest they should be tempted to write upon their personal responsibility what ought to be first examined officially. The churches and the Union will give no importance to such individual unofficial communications, and will not be responsible for them.

2. The Executive Committee are examining the question of inviting the Union to hold its annual meeting this year before May, in order to consider this subject and officially communicate to the Special Committee the facts of the case and the exact points of difference through Mr. Minasian, their representative.

3. Unofficial individual communications, cannot and should not affect the decision of the questions. To the churches belong the questions, and our Union can properly present their complaints.

4. It is requested that the pastors and delegates confer with their churches and come to the meeting with a full understanding of their views.

5. The Executive Committee do not think it useful to publish anything on these subjects in the Armenian papers, and request, therefore, the brethren to avoid it.

THE EXECUTIVE COMMITTEE, BITHYNIA UNION.

To Rev. N. G. Clark, D. D.:   JANUARY 1, 1883.

. . . Meanwhile there had come to us both a pamphlet containing letters from Dr. Hamlin and others as to a difference between the native pastors and the missionaries of the American Board in Turkey. We have carefully read it, and feel that the Board at its meeting in Portland appointed a committee to consider the matter none too soon. We are glad that four of the seven are laymen, because some of the ecclesiastical questions involved may best be looked at by laymen. We regret much the course of Rev. Mr. Barrows, one of the missionaries, in speaking of "the inbred deceptiveness of the Oriental character," as if it could not be uprooted by divine grace, and had not been in the young men who have come to this country. We regret that one of the secretaries has put himself on record as opposing the coming of these Armenians to this country to seek a higher education ; for this is just what the young men of China and

Japan are doing; and if these Armenians are to be leaders of thought in their own country, such an education would be desirable ; in fact, several educated in England and Germany are already very useful in Turkey ; why, then, should not an education here be sought by some of them? Moreover, the words of Dr. Cyrus Hamlin, "I cannot resist the impression that we are in danger of losing the works of forty years," will have and ought to have great weight with the American .churches, who sustain the American Board.   S. M. KEELER,
MILFORD, CONN.   G. H. GRIFFIN.

FROM A CORPORATE MEMBER OF THE AMERICAN BOARD.

NOVEMBER 4, 1882.

Though I have not the pleasure of a personal acquaintance, I presume that I am indebted to you for the pamphlet in regard to the difficulties between the Missionaries of the American Board and the Armenian Churches, which I failed to get when in Portland during the meeting of the Board. I have read it with great interest. I have been long aware that these difficulties existed. I was in Constantinople in 18—, and as a corporate member of the Board was invited to attend the meeting of the Mis sionary Association then in session. I confess that I was a good deal surprised to find not a single Armenian pastor present, and still more to learn, as I did from my friend ——, that none of them would be allowed to attend, even as spectators. My dear friend, Pastor ——, asked me to meet some of the Armenian pastors, and to hear their grievances, which I did, and I have ever since felt that however "wise" Dr. Anderson might have been in the conduct of the Turkish Mission, he displayed a great deal of " zeal without knowledge." In the autumn of that year, at the meeting of the Board, I heard Mr. —— expound and defend what seemed to me his very foolish scheme for the education of native pastors. But as he was backed by Dr. Anderson, opposition to it was then useless. From what I learned in Constantinople, I became convinced that the *Ecclesiastical* relations of the Missionaries to the Armenian churches were both anomalous and absurd. And in the next place, that it was foolish to attempt to transplant the New England Congregational *Polity* in Turkey. Of course not very many Armenian young men can be educated for the ministry in the United States, England or Germany, but it seems to me that those who are thus trained should be sent back by the Board, to serve, not so much as pastors of local churches, but as evangelists, to stir up the old Mother Church. For proper missionary work, a man like Pastor ——, in my judgment, is worth ten men like the one who protested against the Hartford ordination. If our Boston friends did the proper thing they would instantly recall him. The man who could write such a letter has no business to be where he is.

18

TARRYTOWN, N. Y., July 7, 1883.

Dr. Thomas Laurie:

DEAR SIR: When do you expect Pres. Chapin back from his mission to Turkey? I should like very much to see and have an interview with him. I should also like to have an interview with your Com. before you prepare your report to the Board. I beg that you would kindly arrange for the desired interviews, and report to me as to time and place, and oblige. Yours truly,

(Signed.) S. M. MINASIAN.

PROVIDENCE, August 20, 1883.

S. M. Minasian, Esq.:

DEAR SIR: I have notified a meeting of our Com. at the Cong. House, Boston, August 28, at 11 A. M.

But whether they will be able to prepare the report then, or will wait to confer with Pres. Chapin on his return, I cannot say. He sails September 1.

Nor can I say how much time they could spare on the 28th, as there is a great mass of manuscript to be gone over at this meeting. I am sorry to be so indefinite, but I thought it best to tell you all I know about it now, and let you decide for yourself what course to take.* The Lord direct us all. Yours truly,

(Signed.) T. LAURIE.

FROM PASTOR KEROPE.

CESAREA, Turkey, December 9, 1879.

I am exceedingly pained to see the ungenerous conduct of the missionaries in regard to our young men. They always try to keep back our people, and putting themselves forward, dare to publish insinuating stories about us, such as Mr. Barrows does in his letters lately published in America.

. . . . Our missionaries, who always are ready to proclaim themselves to the world as our friends, not only do not show any sympathy or friendliness themselves toward our young men, but show them ill-will, and try in every way to bring them into public disfavor; thus dissuading those who felt inclined from rendering any assistance. . . . .

KEROPE YAKOBIAN.

FROM DR. KAVALGIAN.

". . . . We Armenians notice this caste spirit in our American missionaries in this country, and we feel it very keenly indeed. It is true what the doctor says about intermarriage between the missionary and his convert. Our old members relate a painful story of forced separation between an Armenian gentleman and an American missionary lady who were attached to each other sincerely. The lady was sent back to America almost by force, and the affair was over. This is an old sore, but there are recent cases that we could quote from personal knowledge, if we deemed it needful to speak on this topic. . .

---

* As no definite arrangement was made by Dr. Laurie for the interview requested, Mr. Minasian did not intrude himself upon the Committee.

" I do not know of any missionary that has, or will have, his child baptized by any of our native pastors, but they go many miles to find an American to baptize their children. From among the many scores of missionaries that we have among us, I know of only one lady who is a member of one of our churches. Our missionaries never enter into fellowship with the churches that they organize. We have a young American missionary somewhere not very near to Adapazar. He is a Yankee. Some of the missionaries do not believe that this gentleman will ever be of much use in this country unless he changes his career. He once lashed his Armenian Protestant servant with a horse-whip for a trifling offence. In our late Annual Conference, that took place at the same time with the annual meeting of the mission, while at lunch with missionaries and natives all together, this gentleman did not deign even to recognize one of us. I heard two of our venerable pastors—men that will do honor to any Christian society in the world—say to each other, ' And this young man will sit in conclave with other missionaries to prescribe the ways and project the means that you and I and all of us natives are obliged to work in, without our having a voice in that council, with all our experience and knowledge of the work.' This made a very painful impression on my mind. The doctor is true again when he says : ' Possibly our missionaries may have to make the yet greater sacrifice of caste feeling to living *with* instead of *among* their converts.' I only add they must do so if a better success is desired.

" But this sounds very much like accusing the brethren. God forbid ! I only brought forth some facts suggested by the doctor's letter. We have many respectable exceptions."

FROM THE MISSIONARY REVIEW, SEPTEMBER, 1883.

LETTERS FROM PASTOR SIMON EUTUJIAN, ETC., TURKEY.

As the missionaries and Bro. Washburn are favoring us with their views of the proceedings of the American Deputations and the Armenian Ecclesiastical Unions in Turkey, it is eminently proper and desirable that some of the native pastors be heard also. The following from Pastor Simon will be found timely and considerate :

" The annual meeting of the Bithynia Union commenced May 30, and terminated June 15. It is a great comfort to us that everything was done in harmony and unanimity. We had with us pastors and delegates from other unions of our churches. Our friends—the missionaries—always used to insist that these questions or complaints were raised only by a small clique in Constantinople. At these meetings it became clearly known how utterly mistaken they were in that opinion, as well as in many other things, and in the minutes it will be seen how inexcusable their mistakes were. The reports of the grievances coming from the provinces greatly shocked the feelings of the brethren, the evils complained of being such as had never been seen and felt to that extent in Constantinople. The Executive Committee will try to publish the minutes of their meeting as soon as possible. When they are published, it will be seen that the grievances of the churches are general and the same in kind everywhere, though possibly they may differ in degree in some localities. This fact will also be seen that the Board has not enough to show for the large expenditure made annually within the past fifty years. We have laid everything before the Deputation fully and frankly, and they confessed that there were, indeed, questions which should be *seriously* considered. I am glad that the matter was so fully presented, though we, unlike the missionaries in these respects, were unprepared and *burdened with many cares ;* nevertheless we do not expect much good to result from our interviews. We were in hopes that the missionaries would modify their course, at least for a while ; but we are doomed to disappointment. They will not change their policy, which is altogether inadequate and unsuited to the work of evangelizing the great body of Armenians, especially at the present time, when they have lost their former high prestige, and the people at large look upon them as they look upon the Jesuit missionaries. The expected reform will not be brought about—we could not perceive anything like it in the mouths of the Secretaries. From all we see, the mistaken policy is to be carried on even with greater pressure, if possible, than heretofore. All the efforts of the mission seem to be now, without changing the basis of their position, merely to throw a handful of dust into our eyes; but the brethren are getting educated in these matters, and will not be deceived. You will hear also that the condition of the ministry is becoming more and more deplorable—especially in the provinces, and the churches are being left without pastors. . . . . Dr. Bacon's memory, in bravely defending the weak and oppressed churches of Christ in this land, will never be erased from our minds and hearts. May the Lord reward him. Though the Board's Deputation has shown great patience and gentleness in hearing everything from us, their investigation can hardly be regarded as satisfactory, because they did not bring the opposing parties face to face, or give opportunities for cross-examination."

The following extract from a letter of an Armenian lay brother to a friend in America is also helpful in presenting the Armenian view of the mistakes of the Board and missionaries :

"The mission, you know, has been wrong on the education question. Wrong on church building question. They have been wrong in putting the evangelical communions under a Church polity so unsuited to the genius of the people, and against which they have been protesting from the moment they understood the case. They have been wrong in heartlessly, nay, even scandalously, pursuing their runaway scholars and other young men who came to America for a higher training. They have been wrong in refusing to admit a single Armenian pastor, even the best, even as a mere spectator into their business meetings, and in not putting a single pastor into an equally responsible position with themselves. The policy of the Mission on this point is just as censurable as the policy of the Turkish Government in refusing to place its Christian subjects on equality with themselves. Whatever little advance has been made on any of these points, has, you know, been gained, every inch of it, by hard fighting. I asked the missionaries in 1852 to invite Pastor Der Sahagian, a man upon whose soul the spirit of God had been working before missionaries entered Turkey. You know all the history of Der Sahagian's life—how he was exiled for the Gospel's sake. Afterward he visited the United States to obtain a more complete education, and you know how on his return he cheerfully took up the self-denying labors of an humble country pastor. They refused to admit such a man into the meeting as a mere spectator. My motive in the request was simply to have him gain more experience and more zeal, if possible, in the work."

FROM A FRIEND.

JULY, 1883.

You know that it is hard for men to acknowledge that their policy has been wrong, and if they are publicly attacked their pride is apt to make them stand firm rather than yield an inch. They will be more likely to change their policy voluntarily than if there is an attempt to force them to do it. It is true that they have let the appeals of the Armenians go unheeded for thirty years ; and very likely they would have let them go unheeded for thirty years more, if it had not been for your persistent efforts, and for your pamphlet of last fall, and especially for the blunder which the Board made in attempting to suppress it. Your appeal to the public has been effective ; but the attention of the management has now been gained, and I should recommend waiting now to see what they will do before appealing again to the public. . . .

True that this is a one-sided investigation; there has been no submitting of the matter to the Investigating Committee by our Armenian friends, yet it is possible that the management will propose something that will be measurably satisfactory. If not, our Armenian friends can then appeal to the public as well as now, and will be in a better position to do it if it becomes manifest that the management are not going to do anything to remove the difficulties.

FROM AN ARMENIAN.

There is not a pastor in Turkey, a part of whose salary is paid by the mission, who is not, in the language of the leaflet a " hired helper;" and there is not one pastor who has not been to Europe or America, though he receives no help from the Board, who is independent, and not looked upon as a "hired helper." When a pastor has some trouble with a missionary, who is their judge ? " You must," they say "go to Boston and speak to the Secretary ; as we are responsible to them only." Is it possible to labor with a body of men who recognize no authority, no church, no council, no conscience out of Boston ? . . . They say that some of the churches in Turkey are entirely free from missionary control, as the Congregational churches are free from Home Missionary control. What a blissful state ! Have we come to that ? Is not that the burden of all our requests—to be free from

missionary control, which at times is as hard and heavy as that of the
Turk?

They call the remarks about caste and race prejudice " weak and foolish."
What do you think of the letters of Messrs. Herrick and Barrows? In
private they condemn those letters, but in public they think it foolish in us
to speak of them. Mr. Herrick, in one of his addresses before the American churches, without making any distinction, calls the natives among
whom he is working "domesticated animals; men in whom the human
element cannot be discerned—beasts who use their fore feet in place of
their hands, growing like the wild ass' colt." He is a missionary who was
removed from Constantinople by request of the natives, on account of his
belligerent qualities, and the same missionary by the Board made teacher of
our young men preparing for the ministry.

Rev. Mr. Wheeler, the President of Armenia College, calls the native
pastors his donkeys in his stables crying for food. The church at Harpoot,
on account of such frequent unkind expressions, prohibited him from preaching in their pulpit. He came to America, raised a sum of many thousand
dollars, and went back to thunder from the pulpit that was closed to
him. But what power is there in a native church? All the power is with
the strong.

FROM MR. S. M. MINASIAN.

FEBRUARY 3, 1883.

Incalculable wrong and injustice are done to the feeble churches in Turkey by those who are supposed to be their friends, and we have *no* one
whom we could put forward for their defense. Please read in page 428,
November *Herald*, 1882,* Dr. Clark's statement in regard to the Armenians
who differ from the missionaries in their policy. That statement *wholly*
misrepresents the case. I know of no Armenian who wants " to be put in
charge of the funds of the American Christians." Such charges are repeated
again and again, and everybody here seems to believe them. Dr. Clark's
paper passed through the hands of an honorable committee, who are pre-
sumed to have examined impartially the subject matter, and this committee
voted upon it and recommended to have the paper printed, including the
entire unjust charges against the Armenians. What must we do under such
circumstances?

A deputation from the American Board to the Western Turkey Mission
for information, will not have any good result unless the said deputation
be composed of persons, so to speak, of different politics from that of the
Prudential Committee. Also, it should be guaranteed that the people whose
testimony is taken will not be discharged from the employ of the mission,
or in any way injured, if their testimony or opinion should be against the

* " Natives who are indebted for all the education they have to the agency of the Board, and whose esti-
mates of their own abilities or whose views of mission policy are not fully concurred in by the missionaries
on the ground or by the Prudential Committee, continue to be quite free in their advice and criticisms'
*Some of these gentlemen, if they cannot be put in charge of the work themselves, so far at least as to dis_
burse the funds of American Christians, would gladly bring in other agencies to take part in the work.'*

policy of the mission. I hardly expect, however, that our poor people will be treated with that degree of justice, not to say magnanimity. A friend suggested a little while ago to have the grievances of the Armenian churches presented directly to the constituencies of the American Board. But you know we have not the suitable men able to give their time to such a work, which necessarily would require following up. I am willing and glad to do all I can to deliver my brethren from that sort of a semi-slavery state into which they have been forced by the narrow policy of the mission. I thought that giving the pastors power to vote upon the deliberations of the mission, upon things that concern the highest interests of their churches and the future of the Evangelical cause in Turkey, would lead in time to that deliverance, and that it would raise their status and help to develop their higher manhood, and would also lead to peace and harmony between the missionaries and the churches, by training each party to a mutual respect. Hence my suggestion. Dr. Clark seemed to favor the suggestion and has encouraged it all along, but he makes no allusion to it at all in his letter now, and it appears evident that nothing like it is contemplated. It is not possible for any missionary from a land six thousand miles away, with habits, early training and associations so different, and living apart from the people in exclusion, no matter how devoted and wise he may be, to feel as keenly for and understand as well the wants of the people as those who are of the people themselves and sustain the closest social relations toward them.

FROM S. M. MINASIAN.

TARRYTOWN, N. Y., June 15, 1883.

Joseph Bradford, Esq., Chairman Prud. Com. of the American Board.

DEAR SIR: I read with deep emotion and interest in the *Independent* of June 14th the account given by Rev. Mr. Dwight about the "enlightened Armenians," under the leadership of Dr. Avedis.

I knew Dr. Avedis intimately. I last met him in London in 1878, while he was on his way from the United States to his home in Turkey. He was full of hope and enthusiasm in view of what he was hoping and intending to do, by Divine help, in the way of enlightening his countrymen belonging to the Armenian Church, in things pertaining to spiritual life and to revive scriptural piety among them. I expressed deep sympathy with his proposed work and bade him God speed. I was rejoiced to learn from Mr. Dwight's account that Dr. Avedis has gathered about eight hundred followers with whom he has been working for the regeneration of the Armenian race within their mother Church—a most desirable thing, and a work with which every member of the American Board and all its supporters, as well as enlightened Christians everywhere, would doubtless gladly sympathize.

I regret, however, to learn that there was danger of putting a stop to this good work by these enlightened Armenians being cut asunder from their connection with their church, and I hasten to write this to respectfully ask

24

the Prudential Committee of the American Board, if they deem it best, to
request their missionaries in Turkey, by cable or otherwise, to use all their
influence in the case against the formal separation from the Armenian
Church, and the uniting of the said eight hundred enlightened Armenians
with the Protestant organization, I know that the leading men in general
in the Armenian Church do not oppose evangelical views entertained by
their people. They rather favor it.* Their opposition is wholly against
the spirit of secession from the national organization into which state the
enlightened men often fall, being led by outside influences and unwisely.
I fear that Dr. Avedis may have rather injudiciously and unnecessarily led
his followers to imitate too closely the Protestant forms and usages, and
thus excited the fears and suspicions of the Armenian Bishop, who resorted
to the rather severe measure of discipline and caused his banishment.

In expressing this my fear in regard to my dear friend Dr. Avedis, I do not
mean in the least to pass judgment upon him, for I deeply sympathize with
him in his troubles. I further suspect that the missionaries of the American
Board, being already unfortunately committed to this measure of encourag-
ing secession from the Armenian Church, in the belief that it is impossible
for one to lead an enlightened spiritual life in that church, may have also
exerted their influence, may be unconsciously, to have these "Enlightened
Armenians" clothe themselves too much with the forms of Protestantism
and spirit of secession and thus helped indirectly to bring about the disturbances related in Mr. Dwight's letter. That little body of Armenians hold-
ing Evangelical sentiments, if left to act and work in their mother church,
may prove like the little leaven which will in time leaven the whole lump.
Better, a thousand times better, it would be for vital Christianity in Turkey
to have this body of Armenians remain in their Ancient Church and bear
much persecution rather than to be cut off from connection with their
church, kindred and people. I have no fear, however, that they would be
persecuted long, for the Turkish government, if they remain firm, will be
compelled at last to protect them in their rights to retain their Evangelical
views without being molested. To and for this end let Christians pray
and lend their sympathy. I write as a member of the American Board, and
in the name and behalf of the pure and undefiled religion of Christ our
dear Saviour, and in the hope that the Prudential Committee would in their
wisdom deem it best to take the proposed action in the premises.

I am most respectfully yours,

S. M. MINASIAN.

* "It would be hard to find an intelligent Armenian in all Constantinople who does not now acknowledge
that there are many errors in the Armenian church, and that what is called the *evangelical* way is the *true
way."—Rev. Dr. Dwight in Missionary Herald, May, 1860.*
"The Protestants here have never been separated from the Armenian civil community, and hence the
old Armenians regard them as a part of themselves. They call upon us, buy Bibles at our hands, and come
to our meetings ; so that we have many opportunities to make known the truth to them, which we should
not have if the lines of separation were closely drawn."—Rev. Mr. Barnum in Missionary Herald, March,
1860.

FROM SECRETARY ALDEN.

CONGREGATIONAL HOUSE, BOSTON, July 11, 1883.

S. M. Minasian, Esq.:

MY DEAR SIR: Your favor to Mr. Bradford of June 15th was duly received. You have already heard from him, I believe, that the documents have been passed into the hands of Mr. Hardy, the Chairman of the Prudential Committee.

I now write in behalf of the Prudential Committee to say that we are, with you, very much interested in the statement made by Mr. Dwight in the *Independent* of the 14th of June, in relation to the enlightened Armenians of Cesarea. I may add that this is a matter which was fully talked over at our recent Conference in Constantinople among the missionaries, and with Dr. Clark and Mr. Torrey and myself, as well as with Dr. Chapin and Prof. Mead, who were present at the conference. We are always, as you know, greatly interested in any indications of the presence and power of the spirit of God among the Armenians. As related to this particular case, as you yourself recognize in your letter, and as was presented most emphatically in the statement given of the incident, the significant fact is that the separation of these "enlightened Armenians" from the Old Church was caused by severe and violent persecution. This we regret, of course, but it is a matter which must be met as wisely as it can be met by those who are thus exposed to the persecution. We are praying very much for your friend, and for our friend, Dr. Avedis, that God may guide him wisely, and that out of this seeming trial there may come the very best results for spiritual Christianity. May God grant His blessing to accompany all the efforts which are now being put forth both in the Armenian church and by the members of the Protestant churches, and also by missionaries and by Christian friends, for the increase of earnest spiritual power in the Turkish Empire! You may be sure that the Prudential Committee and the missionaries will do everything possible in this direction. Already there are indications which are exceedingly promising of a bright day which is coming, when all differences will be healed and the whole work will move on to its nobler future.

I write this in behalf of the Prudential Committee, who desire to be remembered particularly to yourself. Dr. Clark is still absent, resting for a time in Switzerland. We hope that he will be back by the close of the next month. I need not add that it gave us extreme pleasure to meet and take by the hand so many of your own personal friends when we were recently in Constantinople.

I remain, in behalf of the Prudential Committee,

Yours respectfully,   E. K. ALDEN, Sec. and Clerk.

TARRYTOWN, N. Y., August 1, 1883.

Hon. Alpheus Hardy, Chairman Prud. Com. of the American Board.

DEAR SIR : The letter of Rev. Simon Eutijan, herewith inclosed,* is the first direct communication I have had from Constantinople since the visits of the Prud. Coms.' Deputation to that city, and as it expresses views so unreservedly on the pending missionary difficulties, from the stand-point of the natives at the spot, I thought it proper to respectfully furnish the Prud. Com. with a copy of it.

Referring to Dr. Alden's answer to my letter of June 15, addressed to your honorable body, I beg leave to explain that in writing that letter, I assumed that the Prud. Com. in the case submitted would feel it to be their duty to use their influence so as to prevent, if possible, a repetition of the mistake which was once made in the name of the American Board. I refer to the setting up, by the missionaries, of the Evangelical party in the Armenian church, into a separate church organization. You are aware that according to law in Turkey, every religious sect means a nation, and every honest and disinterested man who understands this fact and knows how great an evil these so many conflicting sects and petty nationalities are in Turkey, and how great an obstacle to Turkey's real welfare and progress, would seriously deprecate the introduction or adding of a new sect to the many already existing. Dr. Goodell's very expressive declaration in regard to this matter is just to the point, and I quote it here from his " Forty years in the Turkish Empire:"

" Nor do we make any attempt to establish a new church, to raise up a new party. We disclaim everything of the kind. We tell them frankly, you have sects enough among you already, and we have no design of setting up a new one, or of pulling down your churches, or drawing away members from them in order to build up our own. No! let him that is a Greek be a Greek still, and him that is an Armenian be an Armenian still."

Why the mission changed its policy in this matter and took up one so deprecated, is a great mystery to me. To say that the persecution led to the change, seems like begging the question. There was no persecution until the missionaries began the " pulling down " and " setting up" process; besides, it must be borne in mind that the said persecutions were not by the state, but by a religious hierarchy of a *very* limited or subordinate and only temporary power, amenable to the superior authority of the government of the country, when they exercised power over their people beyond simple church discipline. Most of the said persecutions consisted merely of temporary derangement of business—personal violence was *very, very* rare indeed. Out of the forty members of the first church which the missionaries organized in 1846, because of the persecution, as they say, only two were imprisoned for three weeks and one for two or three days.† These

* See page 19.
† Since writing the above, I see by the records that a fourth person was imprisoned and another member was exiled three years before, but all were liberated previous to the organization of a separate church.

imprisonments were on false pretenses, and as soon as the cases were fairly brought before the government, the parties imprisoned were liberated. You further are aware that the setting up of the Evangelical party into a separate church organization did not stop the persecution. The separation thus, as a remedial measure—as the missionaries say it was—utterly failed of its end. I have personally and with heart and soul been in this work from its beginning, and fail to see the good that this policy of separation has accomplished. Had the missionaries stood firmly by their first principles to have " nothing to do " with " pulling down " the old churches and " setting up " new ones, as Dr. Goodell so significantly and in his own native honesty expresses it, we would have had none of the troubles we are burdened with now—we would have had no " vagabond Evangelicals " calling for a *complete* secular and religious organization, and we would have seen more spiritual power in the Armenian church ; and the cost of the entire work to our American churches here might have been less than half of what it has been. I really pity the missionaries and sympathize with them, for this mistaken policy has placed upon them a heavy burden,which they can neither repudiate nor know what to do with now. As to the question that the people themselves asked to be organized into a church, or approved of the scheme, it does not bear a moment's consideration. They were not fit to pass judgment upon such questions any more than a five-year-old boy would be to pass judgment upon any important state questions.

With the kindest regards to the members of the Committee and sincere prayers that wisdom and grace from above may be given them in these perplexing times

I am, respectfully, yours,   S. M. Minasian.

FROM DR. HAMLIN.

Bangor, January 3, 1880.

J. R. Bradford, Esq.:

My Dear Sir: . . . . I cannot resist the impression that we are in danger of losing the work of forty years. The reasons of this impression will appear as we advance. . . . . Two events may be mentioned, among many others, as specimens of those occurrences which have been continually disturbing harmony and introducing discouragements and sourness. The first was the American Board's *change of base* on the matter of education. The Board abolished Bebek Seminary and the female seminary, which had been most singularly blessed in the conversion of its students, and, in the presence of half a dozen Catholic colleges and as many female seminaries, reduced all education to a miserable common-school basis in the vernacular, such as country towns in New England had sixty and seventy years ago ; with this single exception that there was but a limited supply of such trained and sharp teachers as New England then had. This measure at first astounded the native brethren. It was not believed. When it became demonstratively true, anger was mixed with disappointment. I was personally acquainted with some who in consequence went over to the Armeno-Catholics, giving as a reason that the Catholics had never practiced any such enormous deception as to pretend to be the friends of education and then become its real enemies. The choice was a hard one, but among the Catholics their children could be educated in the two or three languages that were more important to them than their vernacular, which was nowhere the language of commerce, trade, industry, the market-place or public meeting. It is true, the firm, consistent, persevering opposition of the native element compelled Marsovan and even Harpoot, after years of useless and injurious resistance, to abandon " vernacular education" as the highest to which man may aspire. Mr. Wheeler's conversion is one of the remarkable events of missionary labor. It seems to be genuine and thorough, but it costs too much. This long contest over education, although the native brethren have won the field in principle, has left a root of bitterness, which has not been eradicated to this day. . . . Another most unhappy event which has had sad consequences, was the attempt and failure of the Pera church to erect its long desired church edifice. A site had been purchased, the missionary church building fund, result of Crimean war bread, contributing a thousand dollars and Mr. Minasian a thousand, which was afterwards increased. The pastor was sent to England to solicit funds. The English promised to do as much for him as the Americans would do, and he came over here, was at the semi-centennial (1860) in Boston, and I translated his address to the vast congregation from the platform. He was coldly received by Dr. Anderson, but he had made a good impression and he felt very much encouraged. Just at this juncture there came a brief letter from one of the missionaries who had opposed the scheme of the church, saying that the money for the church edifice was more than provided for by a national penny contribution in all the churches of Prussia, as ordered by the king ! !

This seemed incredible, the pastor did not credit it, but the letter of the missionary was unimpeachable testimony, and the pastor had to go home, with a little more than his expenses, to find it all a mistake, and not one penny from Prussia. I do not remember how the mistake occurred.

The missionary was honest but hasty, and never stopped to consider how extremely improbable the thing was in itself. He waited for no inquiries and no confirmation, and what was worse, he did not seem to concern himself at all about the results. All this filled the hearts of the whole church with overwhelming sorrow and bitter indignation. It was just one of those things that Satan rejoices in. It was a blight upon all good feeling between the church and the missionaries. I will mention but one topic more as explanatory of the want of harmony and sympathy. That is the sending of young men abroad for their education. The vernacular standard greatly increased the desire of young men to escape from it, and of the churches to have them escape. There was only one thing wanting to intensify this desire, and that was the opposition of the missionaries. This was given in full measure, and the necessary result followed—that is, a *determination* to go.

. . . . In the conflict which has ensued, the native brethren complain that some of the missionaries never treat them as gentlemen ; they know better than we do what belongs to gentlemanly intercourse, and they are sensitive when the missionaries disregard toward them the rules not only of Oriental politeness, but of Occidental as well. If Mr. Barrows had condescended to treat Mr. John Minasian as a gentleman, and had answered his note in a kind, frank, Christian way, that letter would never have come to the *Herald* of Hartford. An Armenian gentleman, a true Christian gentleman, came to me one day and said he had written two notes to one of the missionaries, a reverend man of long service, and that he had answered neither. I replied " he probably received neither." But he replied that the carrier was a trusty person and had delivered them both. Incredulous, I went to the brother myself. He acknowledged that he had received them both, but he *didn't think it worth while to answer them ! !* That went through all the community and was commented upon as *boorish, uncivilized* and above all unchristian Many similar things have happened, trifles if you please, but it may be doubted whether their resulting influence is altogether trifling.

. . . . I think I can best explain the whole thing to you by supposition. If it will not fit in all particulars, it will be sufficiently exact for my purpose. I wish you to suppose that Boston, instead of being as it is, were composed of a population entirely and absolutely without public schools. There are Unitarians, Universalists, Catholics, Tunkers, Hardshell Baptists and Mormons. But each sect has its own churches, school-houses and schools, and is exclusive and bitter toward other sects. Now you yourself belong to a new sect called Orthodox, the smallest and most insignificant of all the sects in Boston. But you know you have the truth and are comforted. You have no church edifice, and, being poor and persecuted, you cannot build one. You hire some place to worship in, or you beg from some of the other sects the use of a church at such hours as will not incommode them. If people ask you about it, you reply : "Oh, we are going to build sometime," and you continue to make that same answer *for forty years.* With your schools you do the same, or even worse. Often you can hire no house for a school and your children are in the streets among the Mormons, or get into Universalist or Tunker schools, and are abused and cursed. Now there is all the time another sect called the *Uniates,* because united to the true Church of Rome. They are numerous, rich, powerful, have noble churches and school buildings; but they speak your language, read your books, have many points of sympathy with you. They have become dissatisfied with Rome because the Pope claims infallibility, which belongs only to God. They hold to the supremacy of the Bible, and are going to renounce Rome.

You now invite them to join you. But they at once reply : "We like many things about you very much, but you are vagabonds ! You have neither church nor school after forty years. You have no central home. You live by begging. Whether it is your fault or your leader's, is nothing to us. In religion you are Gypsies, only you do not own even a black tent." I think after receiving such a reply you would have little courage to invite the Uniates to join you. And when you should hear that they are carrying off with them some of your own staunch friends, and are inviting you all to come with them, assuring you that you shall have freedom of conscience and be incorporated into a powerful body with churches, schools, colleges, high-schools and female seminaries, would you not feel that your little discouraged community is in danger? And most assuredly you would no longer wonder that not one of the Uniates should join you. Now, my dear Mr. Bradford, if you have been able at all to enter into this supposition in imagination, you have, after all, but a feeble idea of the disadvantages under which the Protestant Armenians labor.

. . . . Every young man who has started with a good foundation of English and of character, has done well. I recall at this moment five such cases : 1. Alexan Bezjian, now professor in Aintab College. 2. Alexander Djijizian, pastor at Ada Bazar, who spent one or two years in Edinburgh. He is a noble and strong man in judgment, power of argument, in true insight, in theological training, and as a preacher—the superior of many a missionary. 3. The late Broosa pastor, now head of the High School, who studied at Basle. No one will dare to impugn his character and ability. 4. Pastor Kerope, like the others, a Bebek Seminary student. He went to England, and Mr. Farnsworth, instead of opposing him, had the grace to aid him. He made a good impression in England and obtained aid to build a church, and Mr. Farnsworth pronounced it the best church that has been erected in Turkey among the Protestants. 5. Pastor Thomas, of Diabekir. I do not know of a man who speaks the Armenian language who is his equal for a platform speech. He carries his audience with him. He is clear and logical. He lifts up his audience to higher planes of principle, thought and feeling. I never had a student more easy to be led, more difficult to be driven. Mr. Wheeler undertook to drive him. All his campaigns against him failed, inflicting, however, deep and rankling wounds in the evangelistic work. He is still an excellent and powerful preacher of the Gospel, and should have been a most efficient coadjutor. Now all experience proves that a well educated man of well-balanced mind and character may derive advantage that will be permanent and valuable by one or two years' study in England or America. Instead of uniform opposition let there be intelligent advice, and all these evils will disappear. So long as there is nothing but opposition the evil will increase. Two will come instead of one. Mr. Barrows, or some other one, will vilify them through the press, the whole community will be on fire, and so the pit will be ·digged. It cannot go very much farther. Already the idea is afloat of going back to the old Church, with *liberty of worship*. I am not sure the Church would not grant this, and then both church building and school building would be provided.

. . . . I have written this long letter as one sympathizing with the native body, and with a part of the missionary body. I say frankly, I have no sympathy with the other part.

Their course must end in disaster and ruin, and it is not far from it now.
May wisdom from above be given you to do that which the case demands.　　Very sincerely yours,　　　　CYRUS HAMLIN.

REPORT OF THE MEETING OF THE HARPOOT UNION.
[CONCLUSION.]

By the contents of personal and official information received so far by the meeting of our Union, we have come to this conclusion about the state of the churches in our Union:

That in general the churches now are not in the state in which they were fifteen years ago; that the churches for the most part have neither school nor church building, and of those that exist some are dilapidated, some half-built, and some improper; that generally the churches are poor, and even giving according to their ability have not been able to provide for the immediate wants of the church; that ministers and teachers greatly suffer from material wants, and there have been some who have died on that account; that the churches in general have not only ceased from growing in number but even grow backwards; that the churches are generally in despair, and for this reason some individuals have gone back to the church of their fathers; that some churches have no ministers, their dead remain for days unburied, and there is no one to perform the ceremonies of marriage and baptism; that some churches and ministers are dishonored, scorned and ridiculed and find no encouragement, whereby in this body some deep and incurable wounds have been opened; that ministers withdraw from the work; that the churches cannot defend their rights before the government; that we have no written records—not even the primitive, leaving aside the official; that there is no sympathy between the natives and missionary body.

But why did these things become so? Seeing the results, we are naturally led to seek for causes in that body which before the Christian world has taken charge of this work. And we plainly see that the principles of that acting body are the cause of the present disastrous state of the churches. Behold the causes which our Union with long experience and irreparable losses has found to come into collision with the local good of the churches and to damage them seriously :

I. The officers of the Board, who have officially taken the charge and responsibility of the work, worked with extreme independence and did not respect the idea, opinion, counsel and co-operation of the natives in whatever form they were presented to them with respect to the work which concerned the local good of the churches.

II. They held the work in a vague manner : where there was plainly no hope of success there they started to work, and even after many losses did nor recognize their mistake; and where hope was all apparent, they kept back their hands. Instead of strengthening the work in a centre, they hurried to establish here and there insignificant and nominal Protestant communities, and churches unable to govern themselves.

(For example. In the Harpoot field : Shuntil, Garmri, Tchöteli, Yertming, Sursuri, Körpé, etc., etc., etc. In the field of Palou : Habab, Khoshmat, Abrank, Nboushi, Shnaj. In the field of Arapgir : Dsack, Heynetsig, Mashgerd, etc.)

III. The principle of self-support, which our Union well approves of when at the proper time, the missionaries used before the time, by cutting off their help from the churches prematurely, without having prepared in them the elements necessary for self-support. Before these poor churches such new ways of expense were opened, that the accounts of some could not be closed, even after getting a tithe from the bread, wheat and fuel, which the poor had obtained by begging.

IV. Following the principle of "vernacular" education, the missionaries did not educate the ministers and preachers as much as their high calling and the good of places they went to required ; they sent men to lead churches and communities who had a deficient education, often not able to understand the principles of their mother tongue, leaving aside the classic, which is absolutely necessary for the present. Though now the Armenia College gives a high education, but this "conversion" has been so late, and the ministry is so fallen to-day, that however much we have examined and inquired, we have not been able to find an able young man who should desire to be a minister.

V. The native workers were not encouraged in any way, especially morally, and many times some missionaries showed the native such offending treatment, and wounded the heart of the native workers with such bitter words, that the cure is very difficult and requires a long time. The natives were abused publicly and in private, and even attempts were made to abolish our Union. (Leaving aside unbecoming words said in private to ministers, such as, " Go and eat barley," " You eat from our manger," it was said after the death of a minister who had preached thirteen years, " It was well that he died," etc.)

For the meeting of 1879 of our Union, it was said, " It perished" [like an animal]. Here is an extract from the minutes of that year :

" At that moment one of the missionaries changed the matter to a personal question, and abused the whole of our native meeting, and to him one of the pastors opposing the discussion became so hot, that the meeting was confused, and while there were many questions to solve, the audience, tired and satiated with the abusing and scorning words of the missionaries, cries were raised of, ' Let the meeting be closed,' and the closing of the meeting was resolved." This small portion of that nation which has accepted Christianity since fourteen centuries, and held it for five centuries among Mohammedan peoples, has heard from strangers such words that have sorely wounded their hearts.

VI. The educational establishments, which are few, are in such a position that they are inaccessible to the greater part of the children of the church, and the rich alone are profited by them, while our children grow poor in mind.

VII. The missionaries have not shown a disposition to keep harmony and union even among the churches, and often acted against it.

VIII. They concealed the real state of the churches from the helping churches of America, and often presented it in too bright colors.

IX. When a difficulty arises about any question between the people, or with the missionaries, there is no court with any power to end these difficulties, so they remain unending. If the present disastrous condition of the churches is in any way slighted and essential changes are not made, there is danger that the labors of thirty years in this field will be totally lost.

If the loss had been only a loss of money (both what the Board spent here, and what our people gave, which means more) the thing would not be incurable (may God forbid that it should be so) ; but rational men, bearing the image of God, are being lost. God forbid, but if this state of things remain so, our eyes will at last see that the sun shines upon the pitiful wreck of all our expectations, and to us will remain only a small numbered community, exposed to the ridicule of others and thrown about like dust before many winds.

FROM S. M. MINASIAN.

PARIS, September 19, 1869.

Rev. G. Washburn:

DEAR BROTHER : The long-existing state of the affairs in connection with the missionary work in Turkey, as you know, has often been, to many of the best friends of the cause of Christ there, a cause of query whether Protestantism as a distinct organization should be longer kept up, and also if the ascendancy gained in the religious reformation in Turkey by the Christian churches of America would, or should, longer continue. If we must take the affirmative side of these queries, it would necessitate the introduction of some important changes in the mode of missionary operations in Turkey.

The status of the native laborer with the missionary must be raised, his importance and equality to the missionary in the work must be practically acknowledged. The missionary should not be able to say to a native pastor, who, feeling his ministerial character injured by the former's official acts, appeals to him for redress : "There is no hope of redress for you this side of the water ; as for my official acts, even if they injure your character, I am responsible only to my Board, six thousand miles away." Neither should he be again permitted to say to a church : "Your pastor or delegate in an Ecclesiastical Council of your sister churches voted unfavorably to us, therefore you must repudiate his acts, else, as we are the keepers and distributors of the money, we cannot conscientiously assist you to sustain the institution of the Gospel in your midst."

This state of things ought to be changed, and I trust, as the Commission respectfully recommends, the American Board will send "a deputation to Turkey to visit the churches, confer personally with the brethren, examine the present state of the work, and fix upon the principles upon which the missionaries and the churches are to labor together."

I am not in favor of inciting a subject people to opposition, yet I hold that when they want or ask for liberty it must be granted. The very fact of their asking for it proves that they appreciate and are prepared to enjoy it. May God grant us all the spirit of humility, so that we may daily ask : "Lord, what wilt thou have me to do?"

I remain yours, etc., S. M. MINASIAN.

FROM AN ARMENIAN PASTOR.

AUGUST 9, 1883.

S. M. Minasian, Esq.:

MY DEAR BROTHER : You have already been sufficiently well informed of our doings at the meeting of the Bithynia Union. We had delegates with us from Marash, Harpoot, etc., and all the brethren were unanimous on all points of differences which exist between the missionaries and the Evangelical Armenian Churches. . . . I trust you will not waver in the steps you have taken in behalf of our churches, and pray that the Lord may assist and guide you by heavenly wisdom in all things that you may do for us. The delegates from the Board tried to encourage us, saying that the American Board may introduce many changes or improvements in the management of the mission work here, and that they themselves will do all they can for us in this matter, and advised us to wait and not make further public appeals. . . . I do not feel very hopeful, however, that these questions will be solved in any satisfactory manner, and fear that by conciliatory words they are trying to gain time.

S. M. MINASIAN TO PERSONAL FRIENDS.

They say "the churches are free from missionary control, and they can change their system of church government," etc.

Have they not broken up the Pera church, because that church wanted to change its church government? and have they not starved out the men in their employ who belonged to that "*free*" church in order to bring them to terms? Have they not turned out the Vlanga church and school from the chapel building by police force just because the church elected a pastor whom the missionaries did not favor? The question is not whether the missionaries are praying men, but whether they acted fairly and wisely in these matters, and whether they are presenting *honestly* the points at issue now. I mention these instances because the present troubles are to a great extent the result of the actions of the mission in those days.

We in this country deprecate the pauper labor system of the old world, but our missionaries in Turkey are helping to perpetuate that vile system, not by living as paupers themselves, but by forcing the men whom they hire to do the gospel work to live as paupers.* The plea is that they must teach the people self-support, but really by this course the missionaries are driving away all good and able men from the ministry, and no young man who has the example of these pauper pastors before his eyes ever thinks of entering the ministry. Yes, they may study for a while, but soon give it up.

There are two points in the controversy in which the representations of the missionaries seem to me to be *unfair*. One is, when the Armenian churches ask to have a voice in the management of the mission work, they are represented as claiming to have " control of the funds of the Board." Now I have not seen or heard of a single Armenian who makes such an *absurd* claim.

The next point is this : The Evangelical Armenians have been agitating this question of co-operation for more than a quarter of a century. In 1879, as we were returning from the meeting of the American Board at Syracuse, I remarked to Dr. Clark thus : "We have triumphed in a measure on the education question, and now are going to *fight on the same line* for co-operation, until the delegates of the Armenian churches are admitted into the missionary meetings." We also, since that time, have had special conferences with Dr. Clark upon that subject. They have at last been convinced and compelled to acknowledge that something must be done in that line, and for the last two or three years have begun experimenting upon it. Now, my query is this : Is it *fair* or *honest* for the mission to publish to the world that they have co-operation already, as though they themselves of their own accord initiated it ? Ought they not to tell the whole truth in this matter?

---

* "If I am not mistaken, the highest salary that a pastor receives does not exceed one-quarter of that of a missionary (not mentioning those who get only one-eighth). How can it be that the needs of these two classes of people are so widely different ? Either the missionaries receive very large salaries and do not live as the Christians believe they do, or they starve the pastors."—*Address of Rev. Thomas Bagazian.*

35

FROM THE BITHYNIA UNION, DECEMBER 26, 1882.

We declare that we bring forward no charges, unless it be by an unavoidable implication, and we protest against being called "defamers."

Nor do we see that charges are even implied by the contents of the pamphlet; whether against the Board or its missionaries. When a suffering man brings forward facts to prove the injuries he is meeting, or points out the causes thereof, does he (necessarily) by so doing become a "defamer?"

To speak plain, this seems nothing more than an attempt to make us hold our peace. A beneficiary will not, except under a dire necessity, find fault with the agent of his benefactor. Whenever we attempt to make known our pain, we are sure to receive this slap upon the mouth, and are reduced to silence ; but our feelings are not changed thereby, nor are our pains removed, for the facts remain unaltered, and matters even grow worse.

We have no thought of bringing "charges" against either the missionaries or the Board. God forbid. But if by revealing the actual state of things we should hurt the feelings of any one, or mar the good name of the cause itself, it will give us pain, but we deny the responsibility therefor.

From the very incipiency of these now glaring evils, we entreated and petitioned that a prompt remedy might be applied so as to nip them in the bud. But nobody paid them any attention. Behold ! this is a fact ! * * *

EXTRACTS FROM DR. J. G. WARREN'S LETTER—FORMER SECRETARY OF THE BAPTIST MISSIONARY UNION.

My next step was to place the whole work in Burmah in the hands and under the supervision and management of that body, made up, observe, of *missionaries and representatives of the native churches ;* that body to appoint its own officers, including its treasurer, and make appropriations for all parts of the service, whether relating to education, Bible and tract printing and distribution, the compensation of native helpers, the erection of chapels, etc. . . . The most important end had in view was the training of the natives, of all classes, especially preachers and pastors, to habits of doing business correctly, and to make them ready to take the helm of management in all things when the Union retires, as it must, from that field, finally and forever.

To the plan outlined above, several of the missionaries decidedly objected, one, certainly, as I well remember, even threatening to resign and come home if it were carried into practice. He would not be placed, in any respect, in the hands or at the dictation of his brother missionaries, *much less of the natives,* or of both classes acting in concert. He must be independent of all these : he must be bishop in his own diocese, he claimed. And, Anderson, that is what our missionaries virtually are, and are tenacious of continuing to be. It grows up within them. It grows up around them. It envelops them like the air they breathe. Surrounded, as they constantly are, by dependents, the habits of control and of superiority grow upon them. I am not, in this, arraigning them for judgment and condemnation. I should do the same were I passing my life amidst such surroundings, unless I set a stronger and more constant guard around myself than any person is adequate to. And that is what is the matter. They *control*, as a general thing, kindly, but still *effectually*, the natives.

Watchman, Sept. 2, 1883.

FROM THE CHRISTIAN UNION, JULY 12, 1883.

The missionary convention in Turkey, of which we give a report in another column, appears to us to mark a decided and important advance in missionary operations. It is a distinct and emphatic—so far as we know, the first distinct and emphatic—recognition of the principle, that in spiritual as well as in material philanthropy the end to be always kept in view is so to give help as to promote self-help. The native churches say, the missionaries in this Conference are the chief agency for the conversion of Turkey; we are their helpers; the right of control must be left in their hands; the rights exercised by free Christian churches in other lands must be everywhere recognized as theirs; the responsibility must be thrown upon them; in all our work, whether evangelistic, literary or educational, the same weight must be given to their opinion as to missionary opinion; and as fast and as far as native men competent for the work as preachers, editors, and teachers can be found, that work must be put in their hands. This is admirable. If it is not novel, it is at all events something new to have it put with such emphasis, and by such a body.

We believe that history and Scripture clearly demonstrate the truth that every great reform must be wrought from within; it must be, in a true sense, native and indigenous. The impulse may come from without, the permanent life must be developed within; the seed may be wafted from foreign shores, but it must take root and get its growth in the land which needs the fruit. No tree can be transplanted fully grown. When God would send the Gospel to mankind he sent it through men and by men When he brought it himself, he came assuming a human form, proclaiming it from human lips, and manifesting it in a human life. The first preachers were men selected from the race and the ranks to be reached. When that Gospel was to be carried into Greece, one man was appointed to carry it, and he a man born and bred in a Grecian city; but the work was left to be carried on by native preachers and through native churches. In the subsequent history of the Church, the great theologian of the Grecian churches was Chrysostom, a Greek: the great theologian of the Latin churches was Augustine, a Roman; the great revivalist and reformer of Germany, was Luther, a German; the great evangelists of England were Wickliffe, and Tyndale, and Ridley, and Cranmer—Englishmen. Where in the history of the Church was a country ever truly permeated with the new religious life except as the leaders and teachers were its own sons?

We therefore welcome the distinct and emphatic recognition of this principle by the missionaries and secretaries of the American Board in their work in Turkey, as indicating, if not a new departure in missionary work at least a new adoption and application of a principle very imperfectly adopted and applied in the past. Under this principle each community will not only form its own external organization, but will develop also its own interior life. Between the theology of Christianized Asia and Christianized Europe there may be differences as great as between the theology of Chrysostom and Augustine, Calvin and Wesley; between the worship of Africa and America differences as great as between Oliver Cromwell and Archbishop Whately. This principle, faithfully and fearlessly carried out, will give a new illustration of the truth: many members, one body. For though there may be differences of theology, there will be one faith; though differences of ritual, yet one worship; though differences of organization, yet one Church of Christ. And in each community the theology, the ritual, and the organization will take on that form which will best subserve and embody the spiritual life of penitence, of faith, and of consecration.

Heretofore we have had foreign missionaries and native helpers. If the principles laid down by this Conference are consistently maintained and applied, we shall have in the future native preachers and foreign helpers. The bearing of this principle on the question which has arisen between the Armenian churches and the missionaries we shall not here discuss. That question is indeed a somewhat complicated one. In Turkey every one who changes his religion must change his nationality ; and the organization of a new religious body involves the organization of a new nationality, with a civil representative in Constantinople. The missionaries believed that the Armenian Church could not be reformed ; that converts to a reformed Christianity must leave the old Church and form a new one, and this course has been pursued. The Armenians were of the opinion that this was unnecessary ; but now that this has been done, they demand a complete civil organization of the new churches, with a civil head at Constantinople. They also desire a larger influence and a final control in the entire evangelistic and educational work among the Armenians. On this whole subject we shall await with patience and a good hope the report of the Special Investigating Committee, whose character is such as to give a guarantee that it will be faithful and conscientious, and a promise that it will be wise, and of a kind to be accepted by all concerned.

FROM THE INDEPENDENT, FEBRUARY 1, 1883.

AN INTERPELLATION OF THE FOREIGN SECRETARY, FROM A MEMBER OF THE LOWER HOUSE. BY LEONARD WOOLSEY BACON, D. D.

So scanty is the time allowed at the annual meeting of the American Board of Commissioners for Foreign Missions, for the proper business of that body—so complete are the arrangements made in advance, by those who take control of the affair, to pre-occupy the time with a programme of matters that are not business—that a member who would perform his duty must have recourse to the press. The method has its drawbacks. Through no one journal can the ear of the Board be reached ; and in any journal the discussion must needs go to a much larger proportion of outside observers than if the Board were to be allowed, as formerly, to deliberate upon its own business in its own meeting.

In the few hasty and impatient minutes, which were all that could be spared at the meeting of the Board in Portland for the consideration of questions of vital, one might almost say fatal, importance to the noblest of all the Board's missions, there emerged two or three questions even more important, since they concern the very foundation-work of all the missions. It is a pity that there was not time to put and answer these questions, then and there. But it is better that they should be put and answered here than not at all.

1. What is the exact meaning of it, when the administration of the Board being under discussion, the secretaries interrupt a speaker to announce : " If the Board have not confidence in us, we are ready to step down and out ? " The announcement is received with a round of applause, as if for some heroic act of self-abnegation, or for some escape from impending peril.

1. This cannot mean that the administration are ready to resign. They can't resign ; their time is up, the Board is just reviewing their work preparatory to a new election. If the Board has not confidence in them, they won't be elected ; that's all. They *are* " down and out," and it is only because the Board has confidence in them that they are put back again.

2. It cannot mean that, in case they are not re-elected, they have no intention of making a *coup d'etat*, seizing the treasury, and running the missions on their own hook. Of course they have not. They are not the sort

of men to do it ; and about the time of the annual meeting the treasury is rarely in a condition to tempt any man to run away with it. It can't mean that.

3. It cannot mean that if the Board performs its duty of scrutinizing, criticising, and, when necessary, disapproving the course of the administration, the secretaries will refuse to serve. This supposition is morally impossible.

What can it mean? Perhaps a precedent may throw light on this question.

I remember a meeting of the American Board, at New Haven, something less than half a century ago. There used to be a time for the transaction of business in those days, and the Board had taken in hand some question of policy on which it was proposed to modify the course that had been adoped by its officers. Then uprose Secretary Rufus Anderson to protest against such interference : " If the well-considered plans of the Prudential Committee are to be reconsidered and overruled by this meeting, we may as well hoist all sail and run the ship aground." And this saying, from the altitude of his physical stature and official station, made a deep impression. Presently, the youngest corporate member of the Board arose, and began, with painful slowness and deliberateness of utterance: " This will be my first vote in a meeting of this Board, and I have a great mind to say it shall be my last !" And then followed such an exposure of the arrogance, veiled under the Secretary's poetic imagery, and such an exhibition of the right relation of the secretaries and Prudential Committee as subordinates to the Board as their superior, that it is safe to say that during the remainder of Secretary Anderson's long and splendid administration this particular mistake was never repeated.

Let us hope that we have had the last of this " confidence game " in the American Board. That the Board has a general confidence in its officials —in their ability, honesty and prompt and loyal obedience to the Board's instructions may be inferred from the fact of their election. But to ask of the Board any such confidence in its secretaries and committee as should excuse it from the most searching scrutiny into their doings, and the most thorough review and control of their policy, is to invite it to a dereliction of its duty.

The real question is *not*, Has the Board confidence in its secretaries, but, Have the secretaries confidence in the Board ? or do they mistrust the capacity of that body to deal with the administration of its own affairs, and feel it important to use a measure of reticence toward it on critical questions, and to keep it well entertained with eloquent talk, lest it should get down to business ?

II. What is the meaning of this ? A member of the Board at the late meeting was advocating the report of a committee of the Board on which he served, when he was met by the singular announcement from the secretaries : " *We* had you appointed on that committee." Is not this a little queer ? The member certainly thought he was appointed by *the Board* to study and report upon the administration of its officers; but he is publicly told that he is the secretaries' appointee, as if this had some proper bearing on his duty in the case. The secretaries ought to have an opportunity of explaining this. Is it common for them to manipulate the appointment of committees that are to inquire into their course? Or is it only done on critical occasions ? Is the treasurer in the habit of hinting whom he would like for auditors or for the committee on the treasurer's report ? Just how much of this sort of thing is done ? And if only a little is done, is it not a little too much ?

Far be it from me to question the sagacity of the secretaries in selecting that member for that committee; but it would be better to let the Board manage its own business, however inadequately, than to have the interested party interfere, however judiciously. Since the secretaries claim the credit of having made up a fair and thorough committee on the Western Turkey Mission, they must also bear the responsibility of the make-up of the committee *ad interim* to inquire into the affairs of that mission ; and if it appears to any that in the constitution of this committee there is nothing to give to the public a guaranty of severely thorough work, and something to suggest prejudgments in favor of the secretaries and against the mission churches, an official disavowal of any tampering with the nominations in this case may be needed to see the matter right.

III. Finally, just what does it mean when the Secretary, speaking in the name of the administration, declares what " we are willing " or what " we are not willing " to have brought to the knowledge of the Board ? The occasion when this expression was used at Portland has not been forgotten. A member of the Board, having some very exceptional claims to respect and love and consideration, wished to make to his colleagues a communication of great importance affecting their work. He is a man without ready facility in English speech, in fact a convert of one of the Board's own missions, and one who has shown his grateful love for the mission work by a self-denying devotion such as no man dare impeach. This member, unable to utter himself to his fellow-members by voice, attempted to lay the case before them in print. By a most indiscreet proceeding (however well-intended), the copies of his pamphlet, intended for his fellow-members, were gathered up and secreted, and the secretaries assumed the responsibility of the act and gave their reasons why they approved the suppression of the pamphlet ; why, under the circumstances, they were not willing to have it submitted to the knowledge of the Board, and how, in such and such circumstances, they would have been willing. The pamphlet was one that raised grave questions as to the wisdom or propriety of the official action of the secretaries—questions which any member had a right to raise, and which the Board had a right to judge for itself whether it would entertain ; and for the secretaries to make themselves parties to the act of suppressing this communication ; for the secretaries, present in the meeting for the very purpose of having their official work inquired into ; for the secretaries, the subordinates and employés of the Board, to thrust themselves between the Board and one of its members, and say " We object," or " We don't object," does really seem (unless some explanation can be suggested) to be a very extraordinary line of procedure.

Considered as business meetings, the meetings of the American Board are suffering from too much official management. But it is not the secretaries that are to blame for this altogether ; I am almost ready to say that they are justified in it, as things stand. I want to emphasize my great respect and admiration for these able and faithful men. But none the less I feel bound to expose a public abuse which involves the gravest perils to the noblest and best organized of our great charities, and may easily result, sooner or later, in its loss of public confidence.

And since it is only a half duty to expose an abuse without showing the remedy, I propose to show, in another article, what are the improvements required in the meetings of the American Board, and then to speak of the merits of the questions concerning the Western Turkey Mission.

NORWICH, CONN.

FROM THE INDEPENDENT, FEBRUARY 22, 1883.

THE MEETING OF THE AMERICAN BOARD. BY THE REV. LEONARD WOOLSEY BACON, D.D.

What is the object of the Annual Meeting of the American Board?

Secretary Hayden says (in *The Independent* recently) that the Annual Meeting is "part of a great scheme of operations for diffusing missionary information."

A more common impression is that it is a four-days' prayer and conference meeting.

Another opinion, widely prevalent, is that it is an occasion for procuring large subscriptions of money under the stimulus of high excitement and the pressure of competition.

The last idea of it to occur to the popular mind is that it is the meeting of a responsible deliberative body for the transaction of important and sometimes difficult public business. At the late meeting at Portland, when there were a few minutes of brisk interlocutory debate on a matter of some consequence, it was almost comical to hear the expressions of shuddering deprecation of an incident so calculated to " frow a chill ober de meetin' ;" and one of the younger clergymen illustrated the prevailing notions and quite astounded some of us old men with the information that anything of the nature of debate was quite unprecedented at the meetings of the Board!

And yet, as everybody sees, on a moment's thought, the one reason and "formal cause " of the Annual Meeting is that it is the business meeting of a corporation that calls its officials annually to account, reviews its work for the past year, and determines the policy to be carried out by its executive for the year to come. Everything else is incidental to this. The corporation is made up of godly men, who do not enter upon such business without earnest prayer. The business is of a sort to bring together the eye-witnesses of distant scenes and momentous events and so to " diffuse information." The information thus set forth is such as to touch the deepest fountains of religious eloquence. And, amid the fervors of the occasion, charity opens wide its heart and purse with splendid gifts; but all this is properly incidental to the business of the meeting.

Of late years it has become a settled habit, not only with that vague person, "the general public," but with others who ought to know better, to regard the incidental things as the essential and the essential thing as a dull incumbrance, that has to be tolerated as a matter of form and tradition, but which must be kept in a corner as much as possible, so as not to " frow a chill ober de meetin'." The general public are supposed to find the splendid parade speeches much more attractive than the work-day deliberations upon grave questions, and the meeting must be made attractive to the general public. It is so sweet to sit together in heavenly places that the disciples all want to set to and build tabernacles on the mount. And when hearts are flowing together and money is flowing forth, it does seem too bad to leave this exaltation and come down to business. This is just what Simon Peter thought when " he wist not what he spake."

Now, let me not be mistaken as implying any reflection which I do not distinctly express when I say that this tendency of the Annual Meeting is inevitably promoted by the abnormal fact that the meeting to hear and act upon the report of the executive is substantially arranged for and "run " by the executive, whose report is to be heard and acted on. It is they that prepare the voluminous "special papers," that engage the distinguished speakers to "occupy the time," that see to it that the right men are on the right committees, and that digest the programme in general. They almost *have* to do it; for, apparently, it has to be done and it is nobody's else business in particular. And how natural, how (almost) reasonable that the secretaries and Prudential Committee, knowing in their hearts that the Board's business has been done by them faithfully and honestly, and feeling very sure that it has been done wisely, should forget that it is important that the Board should know this, too, and that the public should know that the Board knows it. How natural that they should like to take a short cut through the business by a general appeal for "confidence," forgetful that just so soon as the Board begins to repose that kind of confidence in its officials the public will be bound to withdraw confidence from the Board.

The golden age of the American Board was the age when it was the forum of earnest deliberation and strenuous debate upon the conduct of missions, shared in freely by the vast body of the honorary members and decided on by the authoritative vote of the corporation. The decadence of the Board—if, as Dr. Todd seems to intimate, its decadence has begun—may be dated from the time when the business meeting was supplanted by a meeting for popular impression. In the long run, the steady support founded on the solid, intelligent confidence of the public in an able and faithful executive, held to rigorous responsibility in the annual public inquest of the governing Board, is a better reliance than the annual spurt of competitive subscription amid the cheers of a mass meeting.

If the Annual Meeting of the Board is to be restored, the first step to be taken is for the secretaries and Prudential Committee, by an effort of faith, to divest themselves of all sense of responsibility for its conduct and for its conclusions. The second step is for the Board to assume this whole responsibility upon itself, and at each annual meeting to appoint its own committee from outside the Mission-House, to arrange and prepare the order of business for the next annual meeting. It is needless to say that such a committee would not act without the most free consultation with the mission-rooms. Whatever subject the secretaries or Prudential Committee wanted to have come up would be sure of a hearing. And, if, at some time, it should appear that there was something that the executive particularly did *not* want to have come up, that would have a fair chance too ; whereas, now, it has no chance at all. Doubtless, such cases are not frequent ; but when they do occur they are sometimes the very cases which it most behooves the Board to have upon its docket.

There seems no good reason to fear that the annual meeting thus organized for the transaction of business would be less really impressive than the meetings directly contrived for popular impression. It does not appear, as a general rule, that people are the most impressive when they are most conscious of trying to make an impression. And in the history of the American Board it does not appear that the great debates, like that at Brooklyn, on the relation of missions to slavery ; at Utica, on the mission schools ; and at Hartford, on the Indian missions ; were less interesting to those whose interest is of most account than the finest modern programme, made up of special papers and set speeches by distinguished orators, with the business tucked out of sight into the odd half-hours. In fact, the papers and the speeches need not be omitted. Without trenching on the time needed by the Board for business, there is room for them and need of them in the remaining time, and in the crowded "overflow meetings." Here the "Information Bureau," proposed by Dr. Todd, would have ample scope, and maps and magic lanterns would come, if necessary, to the re-enforcement of the living pastor or missionary. But the best instruction and the highest inspiration of interest would commonly be found, after all, for the best minds, in the business meetings.

Is it not safe to restore the business meetings of the Board?

Is it safe not to restore them?

NORWICH, CONN.

FROM THE INDEPENDENT, APRIL 26, 1883.

THE STATE OF THE WESTERN TURKEY MISSION. BY LEONARD WOOLSEY BACON, D. D.

I never have approached the discussion of any public question with such pain as I feel in view of the present subject.

Thirty-two years ago, when I traversed the whole breadth of the Turkish empire in Asia, visiting every station of the American Mission then established, it was the fairest and most fruitful field in all the vineyard of the Lord. In the lands of the patriarchs and the apostles and martyrs were renewed the triumphs and the graces of the apostolic churches, and the sowers and the reapers were rejoicing together. How warm the mutual love that prevailed everywhere, between the missionaries and their multiplying flocks! What mutual confidence! What hopes of progress, which, nevertheless, were overtaken year after year by the beautiful reality!

How is it now? We do not fully know. It does not seem that we have been frankly dealt with by the agents whom year by year we have put in charge with our work, with instructions each year to report to us the condition of their trust. But we begin to find out that for these many years the great and hopeful work, in some most important parts of the field, has been brought to a standstill; that the mutual love and confidence between the missionaries and the Mission churches has been changed into a relation of mutual distrust; that in the very metropolis of Turkey there has been exhibited a miserable scandal—the missionaries going to law against their own converts before an unbelieving Turk, for the possession of a paltry bit of real estate; that the building of churches at that great centre has been inexplicably hindered, even when funds have been provided by individual enterprise and self-denial; and finally, that young men of unimpeached standing in the churches of the Mission, coming to this country on their own responsibility, and in the exercise of their unquestionable rights, to seek the highest education, have been pursued by missionaries with detractions and efforts to defeat them in their undertaking. And this course, involving not only detraction but dissimulation toward the young men, has been countenanced at the Mission-House in Boston. The situation may be summed up in the sorrowful declaration of Dr. Cyrus Hamlin, that *the work of forty years is in danger of being lost.*

The distress of mind with which I recount these facts before the public is not relieved by the thought how easily the necessity of this discussion might have been avoided by a different course on the part of the Board's executive. If only they could have apprehended that their business was only to manage the missions, and not also to manage the Board, but rather let the Board manage them; if, instead of turning the business meeting to which they should render full account and look for their instructions, into a four days' prayer-meeting and praise-service varied with a pious auction for raising gifts with the sounding of a trumpet, they had simply rendered their account without reserve and stepped aside to give the Board the fullest opportunity to examine, discuss, decide, with whatever additional light they could get, from whatever quarter; then the discussion might have been confined to its proper forum and the administration would have been relieved of grievous responsibility for a sorrowful failure.

Or even so lately as last October the necessity of this discussion might have been saved by the appointment of a suitable committee of inquiry. But the pernicious usage of letting the executive control the appointment of the committees that are to inquire into their administration has borne fruit after its kind. In the Committee on the Western Turkey Mission at Portland was one member distinguished among the rest as the strongest partisan of the secretaries and the missionaries in the questions between them and the Mission churches and members of the Protestant community —the one having the least patience with any complaint, the least sense of any need of inquiry—the one who attempted to extract from all his colleagues a promise of silence in the meeting when the report should be presented. I refer to the Rev. Dr. Laurie, of Providence. The Committee *ad interim* is made up of Dr. Laurie and six impartial gentlemen. Dr. Laurie, by reason of a brief experience as a missionary in his early youth, can speak with a modicum of authority ; the other gentlemen have no special acquaintance with the subject. I need not say that the conduct of the inquiry is in the hands of Dr. Laurie, and that the facts which will come before the Committee will be such as he shall have collected and digested. Undoubtedly Dr. Laurie will intend to do justice in the case. But he is perfectly positive what is justice in the case before the inquiry begins. Conspicuously, in the Portland Committee, and in marked contrast with the judicial temper, the ample knowledge and the penetrating insight of Dr. Hamlin, he held that the complaints presented by Mr. Minasian in behalf of his fellow-countrymen were worthy of the very scantiest consideration or even courtesy. The vindication of the course of the executive and of the missionaries by the report of a properly constituted committee would have been generally accepted as concluding the question. Such a vindication, at the hands of the Committee as now organized, will not be so accepted by righteous men, who are resolved that the cry of their aggrieved brethren, lifted up over three thousand miles of ocean, in broken English or in a foreign tongue, and coming to our ears, at last, in spite of powerful influences to stifle and suppress it, shall have a full, patient, kindly and impartial hearing. The secretaries were mistaken if they thought that this way of making up a committee of inquiry was a short cut to piece and quietness.

In the few lines of space that remain to me I can speak of only one of the many points of difficulty between the missionaries and the Armenian Protestants, and on that point I must be brief. I will speak of the Armenians coming to this country to complete their education.

The missionaries do not like to have young men go from their churches to America or England for a higher education ; and they have a right to entertain that preference. They do not think it wise; and they have a right to their opinion. They give no aid nor encouragement to such enterprises, and no one can justly demand that they should give it. Some of them have taken pains to write to people in this country, dissuading them from aiding Armenian students—a more dubious right. In some cases, letters of personal detraction have been written concerning these young Christians in a strange land, privately impugning their character in such a way that they could confront neither the accuser nor the charge. And this is, I was going to say wicked, but it is worse—it is mean. And in one instance a missionary has allowed his zeal for hindering these young men in their quest for education so far to run away with his discretion and his conscience as to involve them, together with the whole communion of the Mission churches, in one sweeping charge of habitual mendacity. And

44

this is not only shameful but suicidal. If this is the fruit of forty years missionary labor, we might have saved our money for a better use ; we had better recall the mission and abandon the field. But what, even then, should we do with our thirty years' boasting of the graces of sincerity and truth that adorn our converts, making the name of Protestant the synonym of integrity wherever a Mission church is found ? But this accusation of the brethren is unjust; and the author of it owes it to his own character, as well as to the outraged feelings of an insulted people, to make apology.

But whether they have a right or not to attempt to hinder Armenian young men from coming to America for education, there can be no doubt that this is most fatuous folly. Here have these excellent men for forty years been deepening the impression in the Armenian mind that America is an overflowing fountain of power and beneficence, of civilization, of Christian learning and piety. They have trained up a generation of earnest young men in their high-schools to desire knowledge and the power of doing good, more than gold ; and have done all this within easy walk of a score of seaports ; and now they think that by saying No, they can prevent these young men from seeking an American education. Expedient or inexpedient, this current to and fro has got to flow, and the missionaries might much better be occupied in wisely and kindly directing it than in a futile attempt to resist it. It has got to flow, and as the return current begins to be felt, the missionaries must make up their minds, however reluctantly, to lose that prestige of being the sole depositaries of Western learning which has given them a more than prelatic influence over the Protestant Armenian churches, and must have faith to witness the unquestionable dangers incident to the transfer of direction and control to the hands of their own disciples.

But while there comes an unwise demand from the missionaries, on the one hand, abetted by the Mission-House at Boston, a like unreasonable demand is heard, on the other hand, that young Armenians of approved character, thoroughly equipped by an American education, in all respects the peers, and in some respects the superiors, of American candidates for the mission work, shall be ordained and sent out as missionaries. To consent to this demand is to establish a permanent prelatical order among the Armenians, such as neither they nor their fathers were able to bear. The answer to be made to it is that when the time comes that such a demand can be made the time is already past when new missionaries are needed at all. The mission work is done. Seed time is past. The church and the ministry are established. What more is wanted is co-operation in another form from America to aid the Armenian Protestants in a more advanced work, which the Mission Board, as its repeated protests of *non possumus* declare, is constitutionally disqualified from undertaking.

NORWICH, CONN.

FROM THE VERMONT CHRONICLE, AUGUST 31, 1883.

MISSIONARIES AND NATIVE CONVERTS.

The *Missionary Review* of September, writing of the "American Board's Deputation and Policy in Turkey," as to which it thinks there is room for criticism, takes issue with some points presented in Mr. Dwight's letter, which appeared in our columns July 20th. There is certainly sufficient reason in what the *Missionary Review* has to say to entitle its words to respectful consideration. They are as follows : "We have no time or space here to answer Brother Dwight's letter of June 9th, to the *Vermont Chronicle*, but must suggest a thought on one or two points. (1) Brother Dwight says: ' Missionaries do not become pastors of churches, because they can render all aid, when asked, without such connection, and because such connection would tend to make the churches foreign to the soil.' *Foreign to the soil! Fifty-four ordained missionaries, by being members of the ecclesiastical unions, would make one hundred and thirteen native churches, with six hundred and thirty-eight native preachers, teachers and helpers, and seven thousand seven hundred and thirty-one members,* FOREIGN TO THE SOIL ! will Brother Dwight hold up that idea and look at it a moment ? The presence of these missionaries there, and their absolute control of the Armenian pastors and churches by means of the $245,000 annual expenditure, does not make them *foreign.* But if the missionaries should become members of their church courts, all these thousands of Armenians would become *foreign to the soil!* Really, brother, is not this a little too childish ? Brothers Riggs and Williamson are members of the Dakota Presbytery. Has this made the Dakota Indians "*foreign to the soil ?*" Dr. Wilson, Dr. Murray Mitchell and other Scotch missionaries in India became co-presbyters with Rev. Narayan Sheshadri and other converted Hindus. Did this make those Hindu brethren and the native members of their churches *foreign to the soil?* (2) You expend great force in emphasizing the entire freedom of the Armenian churches from the missionaries. You say : ' The churches of Turkey are entirely independent of any missionary interference.' ' They are so free from missionary control that they can change their system of church government to Presbyterian, Congregational or Episcopal, if they choose,' etc. (What is it now, brother ?) Why do they desire to be so free from the brotherly influence of their best Christian friends and teachers ? (if indeed they do, which seems not to be the case). And why do your missionaries desire such a separate relation to them ? Is it that you may have a more effective control over them by means of the money you dispense to them ? Would common ecclesiastical relations with them in church courts give them an opportunity to bring you into closer sympathy with them in their peculiar difficulties, and hence an opportunity to influence you to an extent you are not willing to be influenced ? Are you not aware, brother, that this separate church relation between your Armenian brethren, which you so distinctly affirm and reiterate, is the most damaging item in all the charges urged against you and the Armenian Board's officers in this case ? Is it not this standing aloof and above the native churches and pastors that is considered as wholly without authority or precedent in the example and teaching of the apostles, and especially of Him, who, though he was rich, yet for our sakes became poor, took upon Him our natures, dwelt among men and became one of us, that he might the better bear our griefs and carry our sorrows ? Do you really take pride in so distinctly and repeatedly affirming that you refuse membership with your native brethren in church courts ? Does not your higher separate position and outside dictatorship, give you a vantage ground for the arbitrary control of churches, ¡ a says, teachers and all the work and interests of your Armenian brethren, by means of the money you dispense to them, such as you could not gain from common membership in the churches and church courts, exercising your Christian functions and charities, and dispensing the board's money on the New Testament principles of Christian fellowship and brotherhood ? You may think this high outside ruling position more agreeable than to come down into common church membership with them ; but will this more agreeable scheme ever succeed in lifting the 1,000,000,000 heathen and unevangelized from their superstitions and debasement to the high platform of Christian faith and spiritual life ? When Elisha sent his staff to be laid upon the Shunamite's dead child by the hand of Gehazi, it availed not. Elisha had to ' stretch himself upon the child, mouth to mouth, eyes to eyes, hands to hands.' Then, and then only, did he succeed in restoring the dead child to life. When the Son of God undertook human redemption, he attempted it not from the heights of his own separate position, divine and glorious as that position was ; and not by the exercise of mere power, divine and infinite as his power was; but he became a man—'a man of sorrows and acquainted with grief,' ' eating with publicans and sinners,'' despised and rejected of men ;' laying aside his divine prerogatives, ' he took upon him the form of a servant, and was made in the likeness of men,' suffering with us and for us that by thus coming down from the heights of God's throne to our state of humiliation and wretchedness, he might lift us into fellowship and union with himself, call us not servants but friends and brethren, and making us joint-heirs with him to all the glory and treasures of heaven ! If we, dear brother, would lift men from sin to holiness as Christ did, must we not follow his example ?"